Biddy Baxter
Edward Barnes and
Rosemary Gill
devised and wrote
the Blue Peter Book

10s

1

Do you recognize any of these pictures?

They've all been in Blue Peter.
Turn to the end of the book
for the answers.

8

2

3

4

6

7

9

5

10

11

12

Hello there!

A lot of important things have happened since our last Blue Peter Book. Things like Peter joining the programme — Petra becoming a great-grandmother — visiting the Tower of London — becoming puppy walkers again with Cindy, our second 'Blue Peter' Guide Dog for the Blind — and seeing a real spacecraft — Gemini X — not on film, but actually inside the 'Blue Peter' studio. But one of our greatest achievements was buying a house to convert into flats for two homeless families. You can read all about how we reached our target and lots more besides, in this, our fifth Blue Peter Book.

We were able to buy our house because you collected 120 million stamps, and according to 'Blue Peter' viewer Andrew Lee, if all your stamps had been put one on top of the other, we would have ended up with a pile of paper 18·9 miles high! Andrew worked this out by calculating the thickness of the stamps and the envelopes they were stuck to, and multiplying by 120 million. We think this deserves to be put in the 'Guinness Book of Records'!

If you watch 'Blue Peter' every Monday and Thursday you might like to see how many of these puzzle pictures you can spot. And don't forget — there's another competition on the last page, and who knows, this time *you* might be one of the prize winners!

Valerie Singleton

John Dooler

Jason

Peter Purves

Patch   Petra

13

All set for action with plastic macs, newspapers, tubs, towels, jugs, shampoo, cotton wool and flannels.

Bathing the dogs

Petra and Patch usually have a bath two or three times each year – with the odd extra one thrown in when they've rolled in some dirt and smell so horrible that a bath is essential. If you have a dog and want to know the best way to bath him, you may find the things we do useful. But whatever happens – don't bath him too often, otherwise the natural oils in his coat may dry up and you'll do far more harm than good.

The simplest way is to use the kitchen sink, or even the bath, rather than filling tubs with water. Sometimes, though, this isn't possible, and whichever method you choose, you'll need plenty of old newspapers to cover the floor, and something waterproof to cover *you* – a plastic mac worn back to front is a good idea.

If you're using tubs of water like we did when we bathed Petra and Patch in the 'Blue Peter' studio, it's best to have two – one for the actual bath and one for rinsing. Other things you'll need are big jugs for the water and for rinsing, small jugs for the shampoo, cotton wool, an old flannel, and some old towels.

6

The elbow test. This is the best way of finding out whether the water is the right temperature.

A small piece of cotton wool in each ear guards Petra against soap and water.

Old flannels protect Petra and Patch's eyes when we wash their heads.

First shampoo your dog's back, not forgetting his tail — and make sure that the lather is rubbed well into his skin.

Lifting the dogs into the rinsing tubs is a time when they're liable to try to escape!

The flannel is used again for rinsing the head — Don't forget that thorough rinsing is essential.

Val hands us the towels while Petra and Patch are lifted onto a thick pile of newspapers.

We filled our tubs to a depth of about five inches. We used warm water, and the best way to test whether the temperature is right is to dip your elbow in the bath. If it feels comfortable it will be fine for your dog. If the water is too cold, or too hot – as well as hurting him it could frighten him so badly that he'll never want to have a bath again. By the way – before you fill the tubs, make sure you've put a thick layer of old newspapers underneath. Even with a well behaved dog, bathing is always a messy operation, and the newspaper acts like blotting paper and soaks up the puddles.

After taking off their collars (a soaking in warm soapy water is bad for the leather) – we lifted Petra and Patch into the water – talking to them all the time to reassure them. Val was close at hand to help if one of them decided to make a dash for dry land – and you'll find it useful to get a friend to help you, too. A wet, slippery dog with no collar can be a bit of a handful for one person to manage. We also put small pieces of cotton wool into Petra and Patch's ears. This was to make sure that no matter how obstreperous they were, no water would get into their ears.

The first part of your dog to wash is his back and legs – always leave his face until last. But before you apply the shampoo, wet his coat thoroughly with the water. When this is done, he's ready to be lathered. There are many shampoos that are suitable for dogs, but if your dog has dandruff or fleas or any kind of skin trouble, ask your vet for one that is medicated. Rub the shampoo well into his skin – and cover his whole body with lather – including his tail. We put old flannels over Petra and Patch's eyes before we wash their heads. This helps you to make certain that no soap gets into the wrong place.

One of the most awkward parts of the bathing operation is transferring your dog from the bath tub to the rinsing tub. Now's the time you'll be glad of your plastic mac and the newspapers on the floor. This is also the time when your dog is most likely to make a dash for freedom. When he's lifted out of the bath tub he thinks it's all over, but rinsing is of vital importance. It is

Drying takes ages – but it's important for your dog to be completely dry before you let him go.

Patch enjoys the hair dryer. There's no doubt that after his bath his coat looks in splendid condition!

essential that no trace of soap remains in your dog's coat, and this is where the jugs of water – and your friend come in. Jug after jug of water has to be poured over your dog until all the suds have gone. We needed about twelve jugs full for both Petra and Patch, and Val was kept very busy refilling them.

The flannel is used again when you rinse your dog's head. Hold it firmly over his eyes while you pour clean water over it until – like the rest of his body – there's no trace of soap.

When Petra and Patch were thoroughly rinsed, Val was ready with the towels. We lifted the dogs out of the tubs onto a really thick wadge of newspaper and quickly wrapped the towels round them. We had two towels for each dog and after taking out the cotton wool from their ears, we rubbed them until our arms ached.

It's extremely important to make sure your dog is absolutely dry before you let him go. A hand held hair dryer is an excellent way of finishing off the drying. Patch particularly enjoys this, especially when it's blowing warm air.

Because bathing is so messy, some people think that the ideal place to do it is out of doors. But this can only be done on a really hot day when there is hardly any wind. And there's always the danger that your dog will leap out of the bath and into the garden. This is what Petra did several years ago. She waited until she was being rinsed – gave a mighty wriggle and a leap – and ran straight into a pile of lawn clippings. She rolled over and over in the grass before she could be caught, and when she was finally captured – there was nothing for it but to start bathing her all over again!

Ski Story

Being in the 'Blue Peter' studio twice a week makes it very difficult for us to get away during the winter – so when they suggested that we went to Austria to make a ski-ing film, my first question was – 'When?'

I had never skied before in my life, but I managed to get to the bottom of the nursery slope in a more or less upright position.

We arrived at the village of Lech, 4,700 feet above sea level and looking quite breathtaking in the crisp, clear winter sunshine.

We were at the summit of the Ruvikopf, 7,709 ft. up. It was like being on the roof of the world.

'Between the Thursday programme and the Monday programme,' they said, 'so there's no time for hanging about.'

Everything was arranged for a split second schedule.

5.19 p.m. On the air. We say 'Goodbye – see you on Monday' and tear out of the studio.

5.20 p.m. Into the fast car waiting, with engine running, outside the 'Blue Peter' studio. Back in the studio – Editor, Biddy Baxter and the 'Blue Peter' ship appears on the screen.

5.45 p.m. Arrive at London Airport. John thinks he's lost his passport – finds it just in time.

5.46 p.m. Last call for Flight 506 to Zurich.

6.15 p.m. Airborne. London a million tiny lights below us, we head for the Continent and Switzerland.

7.30 p.m. A sleek, black Mercedes picks us up at Zurich Airport and roars off into the night, through the twisting mountain roads, to the Austrian border.

Friday

1.00 a.m. The car crunches to a stop in deep snow outside Hotel Dundhof in the village of Lech, 4,700 feet up in the Austrian Alps. We all have hot chocolate and go to bed.

That was quite enough excitement for one day!

The next morning I looked out of my bedroom window to a clear blue sky with the sun shining down on the great snowy peaks of the Austrian Alps. We were unbelievably *there*.

Before filming could start, we all had to be fitted with skis and ski-boots. Fitting is very important because a wobbly boot can easily end up with a broken ankle inside it. John and I were soon fixed up, but Peter has such big feet that they had to send to the next village for a giant pair of ski boots.

I had skied before, several times, but I was dreadfully out of practice. The great trouble about ski-ing when you live in England is that you never get enough practice. Each year, at the end of a holiday, I feel I'm really getting somewhere – and then, twelve months later, it's like starting all over again. At least Peter and John couldn't complain about being out of practice, because neither of them had ever been *in* practice. They'd never skied before in their lives. But Peter had a good natural sense of

After a day on the ski slopes, the journey back to the hotel is made on a two-horse open sleigh.

Herr Walch, our ski instructor, took me up the slope by T-bar.

balance, and what John lacked in experience, he made up for with lunatic courage. We had a super ski instructor called Herr Walch who gave us the most marvellous encouragement. Whenever we did the slightest thing right he gave delighted shouts of 'Jawohl!' and 'Wunderbar!'

The Austrian children made us seem real beginners, though. They learn to ski as soon as they learn to walk, so by the time they're eight they look like international champions compared with us.

One thing all skiers have in common – from Olympic gold medallists to the novices on the nursery slopes – is that they never know when to stop. At the end of every run they say 'I'll just have one more – and this time I'll really be good.' It's only darkness that sends a skier back to his hotel.

We went back by horse-drawn sleigh through the deep pine forest and over the little wooden bridge that led to the village. Steaming hot chocolate was served before a roaring log fire, and after half an hour we felt so stiff we thought we'd never walk again!

But the following day we were out on the slopes

again as soon as it was light, and this time Peter and John were both able to make 200-yard runs before the sun came down. We also made a trip by cable car to the summit of the Ruvikopf which towers 7,709 feet above the village of Lech. It was like being on the roof of the world. On every side there were snow-capped mountains stretching away as far as the eye could see. The crisp snow came up to our knees, but when the sun shone I could feel it burning my face and the back of my neck.

The sun was still shining when we got up the next day. We had our last ski before a rapid lunch, and then it was into the black Mercedes again for another hair-raising trip along the mountain roads.

We made Zurich Airport on time, and soon we were 30,000 feet above the shimmering mountains, and heading for home. In 24 hours we were back in the 'Blue Peter' studio ready for Monday's programme. Before long we were saying 'See you on Thursday – Goodbye.' But this time we *didn't* dash for a waiting car. We went home through a thin cold London drizzle – the clean crisp air and the towering mountains seemed a very long way away.

11

The best Christmas tree of all

1 It was Christmas Eve, and the snow lay thickly on a little house in the mountains. Inside the house lived Albrecht, and

2 he was very worried. His mother was ill, and they had little food left and no money. But suddenly he had an idea —

3 between two great fir trees, a little one was growing. 'I'll take it to town and sell it for a Christmas tree,' he decided.

4 The market was crowded for the Christmas fair. There were decorations and presents, and all kinds of mouth-watering foods.

5 Lots of people were buying beautiful Christmas trees — but Albrecht's was far too small to be noticed.

6 As night came, he trudged sadly home. No one had bought his tree.

7 'I'll just have one last try,' he thought, as he stopped at a brightly lit house.

8 Inside, the Eilders family were hanging gay decorations on an enormous tree. Albrecht's heart sank — his last chance was gone.

9 But the Eilders were kind. They bought his tree and gave him food, and sent their big dog, Boris, to guard him through the night.

10 Quickly, Albrecht went back to the market and bought a present for his mother —

11 When she saw it she was delighted. Thanks to the Eilders they would have a happy Christmas after all!

12 On Christmas Day, Albrecht took Boris back. 'We've just planted your little tree,' the Eilders children cried. 'Now come with us to hear the carols.'

13 So they all sang carols together and the Christmas bells pealed far and wide.

14 But when they came out, they could hardly believe their eyes —

15 The little tree that Albrecht had sold to help his mother, that the children had planted to save it from dying, had grown into the Best Christmas Tree of All.

BLUE PETER HOUSE

'120 million stamps in four weeks,' Peter said. 'You must be joking!'

But Valerie was perfectly serious.

'We were successful with Honey, our guide dog,' she said, 'and the tractor for Africa – and what about the Inshore Rescue Boats – we got four of those!'

'But this is twice as big as anything we've attempted before,' John said.

'Can you *imagine* 120 million stamps?'

This would mean buying an old house and turning it into two new self-contained flats. The cost – 120 million used postage stamps.

The question everybody asked was: 'What will happen to the stamps, and how will they be converted into money?'

The answer was quite simple. We sell them to stamp dealers by the pound, and they sell them, by the packet, to stamp collectors all over the world.

December 4th was the date fixed to launch the appeal. We asked you to send your stamps to a special address. The next day, we set out through the first winter snow wondering what, if

For four weeks the volunteer helpers worked day and night ripping open thousands of parcels and sorting literally millions of stamps!

At six minutes to five on December 28th, just before 'Blue Peter' went on the air, a message was flashed from the control room to the waiting studio below.

'Light up the chimney on the Model House. The "Blue Peter" viewers have done it again.'

P.S. On 16th March, 1968, there was an auction at Stanley Gibbons, the world famous stamp auctioneers. Lots 201–210 were complete albums of stamps that had been sent by 'Blue Peter' viewers. The money from the auction was put with the money raised from stamps collected since December 28th, and on March 21st we announced on 'Blue Peter' that altogether we had raised enough money to buy *two* 'Blue Peter' Houses – and we were well on our way to a third.

'Can *you* imagine nine million "Blue Peter" viewers ripping stamps off every letter they can find?' said Val. 'Because I can.'

So we decided to go ahead with our most ambitious plan to date. We were going to ask you to provide homes for two of the many thousands of homeless families in Great Britain.

anything, had arrived at our stamps depot. We needn't have worried. The first thing we saw was a policeman sorting out a traffic jam caused by eight large vans, packed to the doors with sacks of stamps.

P.P.S. Even Val was surprised at that!

Joey off duty

'Whatever happens,' we were told, 'don't let Joey get bored – once a parrot feels lonely or has nothing to do, he'll start to pull his feathers out.'

Well, we certainly didn't want a bald parrot, so that was why we decided Joey had better come and live in the 'Blue Peter' office. Here, with telephones ringing, typewriters clattering, and a constant stream of visitors, there would be no chance of him being lonely – we didn't think he'd be bored either. And we were right! It wasn't long before Joey felt perfectly at home – in fact, we have to be very careful that he doesn't take over the whole office. On several occasions he's managed to cut off long distance telephone calls by sitting on the telephones; and before we moved his perch, he chewed away the wooden frame of a large notice board!

Joey's incredibly noisy and not at all tidy with his food. We have to keep a special brush and pan to clear away the empty shells and chewed up bits of apple. And when he decides to have a bath, we all keep as far away as possible because he shakes his watery feathers just like a dog.

All the same, living with Joey has taught us a lot about Brazilian Blue Fronted Parrots. His habits are as regular as clockwork – and we can almost tell what time it is when he has his twice daily naps and his three meals.

But most important of all – our plan has worked – since coming to live in the office, Joey hasn't pulled out a single one of his feathers!

Flying the flag – and surprising visitors to the 'Blue Peter' office.

Mountaineering – drawer by drawer Joey scrambles to the top of the filing cabinet and reaches his favourite woolly ball.

Tea time – Joey prefers his from a plastic spoon.

Train spotting . . .

Typing . . .

Tying knots . . .

Telephoning . . .

FROM: BIDDY BAXTER	EDITOR (Producer)	FOR PROPERTY MASTER'S USE ONLY				
ROOM No. E.514 PABX: 4535		COPIES TO			MEMOS TO	
SUBJECT: Property & Drape Requirements		Producer (3)	✓ Serv. Asst. Props (5)	✓	Catering	x
TO: Property Master T.C.		Designer	✓ Drapes	✓	H/Engineers ᴍ	✓
		Scene Master (2)	✓ Armourers	x	H/Electricians	✓
		Asst. Properties	✓ Designer Ealing	x	Sound Maintenance	x
		Petty Cash	✓ A/Scene Master (EAL)	✓	House Services Man	x
			Booking Clerk	✓	(For Fireman)	x

DESIGNER: Jennifer Wyatt – 2459	SCENIC SERVICING PROD. No.	DATE REC'D: _____ DATE DUE:
PRODUCTION: "BLUE PETER" 3318/1113		Reh. Room Tel. No.

SETTING DATE	S	FILMING	S	REHEARSAL	S	TRANS/V.T.R.	S
o/n setting 13 – 14th	D L.G.	5.3.68	D L.G.	14.3.68	D L.G.	14.3.68	D L.G.

ORDER No.	H	T/C

– 1 –

1. 1 Merryweather fire engine from:
Oxford Fire Brigade HQ.,
Oxford Fire Station, Oxford. Tele: Oxford 42224
VALUE: £500

12' long, 6' wide, 8' 6" high. Being brought to
LGS Prop dock on 13.3.68 and to be in studio by
9.30 a.m. on Thursday, 14.3.68. Being returned
to Oxford Fire Station on Friday morning, 15.3.68.
Movement Control providing transport.

1 pair of grey horses, fully practical, with traces
etc. to pull item 1.

TALL ORDER!

'Ask Bob to get a vintage fire engine.'
'Ring Bob and see if we can have a fish pond with a fountain and 27 tropical fish.'
'Tell Bob we'll need six suitcases for the Hover Pallet, and three bunches of bananas for the elephants.'

It may sound like the world's strangest shopping list, but you can't surprise Bob Sutton, 'Blue Peter's' Properties Assistant.
You can demand a skeleton, or 750 bars of chocolate, or 49 watches and a smuggler's waistcoat, and Bob won't raise an eyebrow – in fact the only time he's really been foxed was when we wanted fresh parsley in December!
Helped by a whole army of behind-the-scenes workers, Bob plays a vital part in making 'Blue Peter' happen.
His job is to make sure that all the things demonstrated by Valerie, John and Peter arrive at the studio on time. And not only the big stuff like the Merryweather Fire Engine, or our train layout –

Choosing a cactus to decorate the 'Blue Peter' studio.

Miles of tables, acres of chairs – there are over 5,500 items in the underground furniture store.

'SMALLS' include anything from six-foot wedding cakes to drawing pins . . .

statues of all shapes and sizes . . .

enough plates for 90 banquets . . .

hundreds and hundreds of telephones . . .

Bob orders every saucepan, plate and spoon that Val uses when she is cooking; all the toys for our shelves; the hammers, nails, drills and paint used by John and Peter; and the food for Petra, Patch, Jason and Joey – and any other animals that are in the programme. The list is endless and it all starts in the 'Blue Peter' office.

When we decide what we're going to do in each programme, we have to write down all the things we'll need. This list, or 'Properties Requirements Sheet' is sent to Bob's office where he and the 'Blue Peter' designer decide how they can most easily obtain the things we've asked for.

Working in television is like working in an enormous factory. Everything has a code or special name and the items on the Properties Requirements Sheet are divided into H for Hire, T/C meaning obtainable from the B.B.C.'s huge props store at the Television Centre, DRAPES meaning curtains, or specially made loose covers, and P/C – things to be bought with petty cash.

Now Bob's detective work really begins. Tracking down the items that have to be hired means telephone calls to antique dealers, large stores or museums, and sometimes the designer will ask Bob himself to choose whatever we need. If we want trees and grass for a garden scene, Bob will have to visit the firm specializing in the hire of 'greenery' – and he may have to call on pet shops and zoos if we need rare animals or birds.

But Bob doesn't have to travel so far afield for everything on the list. Beneath Television Centre lies a rabbit warren of rooms and corridors – looking exactly like a gigantic furniture warehouse.

Here Bob can order what he wants from 2,272 tables, 1,125 dining room and kitchen chairs, 554 arm chairs, 380 stools, 82 desks, 67 sofas and 20 wardrobes. Each one of these has a number, and when a chair or table is chosen, Bob adds the number to his Props Requirements list. This means a check is kept on what's in stock and what is being used in the studios. Apart from furniture and anything on wheels, all other 'stock' items come into the category of 'SMALL PROPERTIES' or 'SMALLS'. There are hundreds and thousands of 'smalls' from drawing pins to six-foot wedding cakes – far too many for anyone to attempt to count and catalogue, but to help Bob and the other Properties Assistants they're displayed in sections looking like a weird supermarket with no prices.

Nothing is forgotten and nothing is impossible to obtain.

There is even an Armoury section with weapons ranging from poisonous New Guinea Blow Pipes to Crossbows and Colt 45's. Here the strictest security regulations are enforced. Guns have to be signed for in a special book and are delivered to and from the studios in padlocked strong boxes.

If we ever need curtains or loose covers, Bob visits 'DRAPES'. Yards of material – plain, patterned and all colours of the rainbow – hang from the ceiling, as well as a vast selection of ready-made curtains.

A team of experts is on hand to make or alter anything that is ordered – and this includes making loose covers for sofas and arm chairs. And if you think sewing is for girls, you'll get a shock. In Drapes, all the machining is done by men – and they're very good at it, too.

The next piece of organization is checking out everything that has been ordered for the programme, and transporting it to the 'Blue Peter' studio. The B.B.C.'s central check point is 'Movement Control'. Here, for twenty-four hours – day and night – vans, trucks, trolleys, cages and lifts converge. Everything hired arrives by van – and is labelled and given a special number. Giant lifts carry trolleys and trucks of furniture up from the basement. The 'smalls' are loaded into padlocked cages, and also arrive by lift – and every single item has to be checked before it is sent to the studio by truck or lorry.

But that's not the end of the story – when 'Blue Peter' comes off the air at 5.20 every Monday and Thursday, everything we've used has to be sent back to its store and all breakages and any damage reported.

And working on 'Blue Peter' there's hardly any time for a breathing space. First thing the next morning the telephone rings – **'Bob, can you get us ten white mice and a helicopter?'**

The 'SMALLS' in their padlocked cage are checked into Movement Control.

In the Armoury – these poisonous blow pipes come from New Guinea.

Bob orders some curtains from 'DRAPES' – there are over 700 to choose from.

The Merryweather arrives, and Bob sees it manoeuvred into the 'Blue Peter' studio.

Tricks and illusions

There's no prize for guessing how this trick was done — it was all done with mirrors! But here are some tricks and optical illusions that may surprise you. Try them out on your friends.

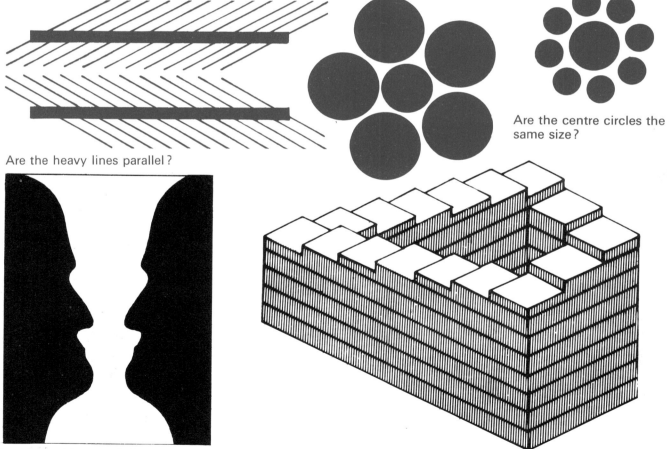

Are the heavy lines parallel?

Are the centre circles the same size?

Is this a white vase? Or two black faces talking to each other?

The impossible staircase. This looks like an ordinary block of stairs — but it would be impossible to build. Start on the front step and let your eyes 'walk' up them. You're in for a surprise!

Tricks with cups

Picking up cups with a balloon is easy!

Blow the balloon up a little way and press the cups against it. Finish blowing up the balloon and when you pick it up you'll find the balloon has stuck quite firmly.

Can you balance a cup on your finger tip?

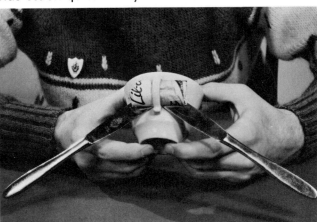

Here's how you do it. Find a light weight cup and two knives with heavy handles. Fix the knives in place with a roll of paper.

Joey's magic cage

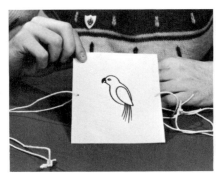

Draw Joey on a piece of thin card and tie a piece of thin string to each side of the card.

Turn the card over and draw a cage on the back.

Hold the card up to your eyes. By twirling the string very fast so that the card spins, you can make Joey go into his cage.

The Blondin card

Here's a famous trick to mystify your friends! Take a card and –

–balance a full wine glass on it. Your friends will be amazed!

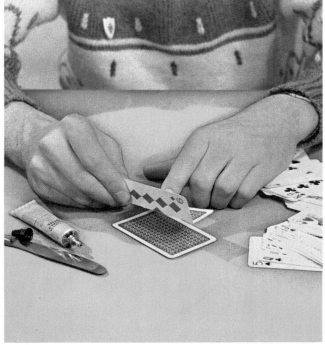

Here's the secret of the Blondin card! – Score half way through a playing card so that it bends easily. Glue half of it face down to the back of a second card. Make sure the edges match exactly.

As you take the card from the pack, secretly push the flap out with your thumb. Practise carefully and your friends will not see how this trick is done.

Miniature gardens

If you haven't got a garden of your own you could make miniature gardens to keep indoors. You can use real twigs and flowers or plastic ones that last for ever. I've made two kinds – one for summer and one as a Christmas decoration

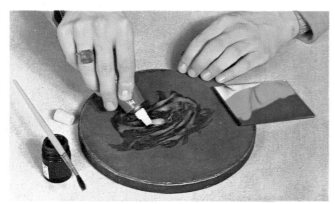

1 The base of my garden is a round cake board. A good size is one about 8 inches across. Paint it with brown poster paint to look like earth and glue a handbag mirror in the middle for the pool.

2 Press a lump of modelling clay on to the board by the mirror. If you're not using real plants you can make a tree by wiring small plastic leaves onto a twig. Push the stem of the twig firmly into the clay.

3 When the trees are in place you can hide the modelling clay with some biggish stones.

4 You can make the grass from moss. If you can't get real moss you can get dry moss from a shop. Put some glue on the board and fix the moss in small clumps until it is covered.

5 I've put some big toadstools in my garden. They're made from buttons glued on to corks. Paint the buttons in bright colours and leave the corks plain.

6 The small plastic flowers are pushed into little blobs of clay and pressed on to the board. Add one or two animal ornaments or toys and your garden is finished.

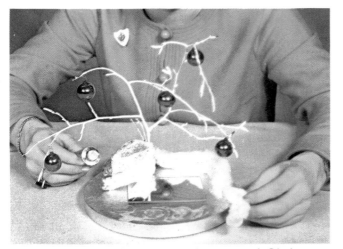

7 A snowy garden can make a good Christmas decoration. Leave the cake board silver and use cotton wool instead of moss. Paint the trees white and hang tiny decorations on them.

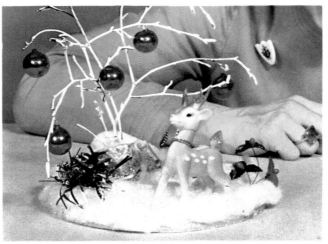

8 I've finished my Christmas garden with plenty of glitter, a little reindeer, and some holly from the Christmas cake.

Bleep & Booster

Bleep and Booster woke one morning to an eerie silence. Miron City lay motionless – with every vehicle and spaceship trapped in a vile green drift.

'What is it?' whispered Bleep anxiously, as Booster scraped a handful of the stuff off the window sill. His hand froze.

'Cheer up,' he cried. 'It's only snow! We have white snow on earth, but yours is green! It's nothing to be frightened about.'

At that moment the Captain came in.

'I'm not so sure,' he said gruffly. 'Snow is unknown on Miron. Our Leader has ordered Phase I of a general emergency. The source of this snow must be discovered.

'I know all about snow,' said Booster, eagerly. 'Let me make a reconnaissance – Bleep can pilot for me.'

'Very well,' said the Captain, 'but keep radio contact and take no chances.'

'What a fuss,' thought Booster as he climbed on board an All Weather Pod which had just been freed from the green snow drift. Soon Bleep and Booster were skimming over the green slopes. At first, Bleep was a bit scared, but he soon felt the excitement of driving through deep drifts, with green spray shooting in great plumes behind. 'I told you,' cried Booster – 'there's nothing frightening about snow!'

Then, without warning, a fierce blizzard started to blow. Within minutes, driving snow had clogged up the air intakes, and the All Weather Pod came to a halt, its jet motors silent.

'We shall have to get out and free the inlets,' said Booster.

As they jumped out into the driving storm, they became aware of a strange sound – a deep moaning which rose and fell evenly, quite different from the sound of the wind.

'Generators,' said Bleep briefly – and suddenly Booster felt scared! The sound seemed to come from inside a large crater, and cautiously the boys crept towards the rim.

'I'll radio base,' said Bleep, and Booster watched anxiously as his friend switched on his personal transmitter, but before even a faint Bleep Bleep signal went out across the frozen waste, green ice formed on the controls. With a sharp crack, the metal contracted and the solar cell batteries lay shattered on the green snow.

'We are on our own now,' said Bleep grimly.

At that moment they sensed danger! At first there seemed to be just the slightest movement of the snow around them. Then, to their horror, silent green forms rose up from all sides – the boys found themselves staring at a ring of icy green inhuman faces.

'The Ice men of Phantos!' whispered Bleep, and he was shaking with fright!

The Ice men closed in slowly, forcing the boys to walk up the sides of the crater to its rim. And there they saw the source of the strange sound. An immense prefabricated circular construction filled the empty crater. From its roof soared a set of giant vanes covering every section of the sky, while from within came the deep moan of generators.

'Snow machines,' said Bleep grimly. 'These evil Ice men are deliberately making snow to cause havoc on Miron.'

There was no time to see more. Ringed by the Ice men, Bleep and Booster were hustled down into the crater and through a narrow entrance into the building.

Inside, they shivered with cold, and in the eerie green light they could make out a vast control room, filled with complex panels, at which sat the still forms of other Ice men.

One of them seemed to be receiving instructions from a computer. Booster knew that the flickering signals were spelling out their fate, and that it was bound to be an unpleasant one.

His fingers tightened around a small metal object in his pocket. It was a small signal flare. Most Mirons carried one or two when they went on expeditions into wild country, and Booster had been well trained. With one movement, he drew the grenade from his pocket — withdrew the pin and lobbed it.

There was a whoosh of bright orange as the flare ignited and spluttering sparks cascaded in all directions.

Fire! — the one thing which Ice men dreaded most had landed in their midst. Panic stricken they broke and ran.

'Quick, Bleep, follow me!' shouted Booster. He dived through a small open door with Bleep close on his heels and bolted it behind them.

They found themselves in a large room with humming computers lined up in orderly ranks.

'This must be the main refrigeration plant,' said Booster. 'Remember, cold is as vital to these people as oxygen is to us. We must put this lot out of action.'

Frantically they threw the switches and ripped the wires from the wall, until, with a few metallic clicks, the humming ceased, and the cold lost its icy edge.

'Look there!' cried Bleep in alarm. The metal door through which they had escaped was now glowing a dull red.

'The whole place is ablaze!' shouted Booster. 'Those Ice men dared not go near the flare to smother it.' A thin metal ladder snaked through a manhole in the ceiling. With fear acting as a spur, they mounted hand over hand upwards, into what seemed an endless black tube. Just as their tired muscles were refusing to do more they tumbled out into clear cold air.

The tube had led them to a small service platform among the big induction vanes on top of the building. They were trapped!

Already the flames were darting hungrily over the domed roof. Escape seemed impossible.

Bleep tried to be brave. 'At least I feel warm for the first time today,' he said cheerfully, but Booster could think of no funny reply.

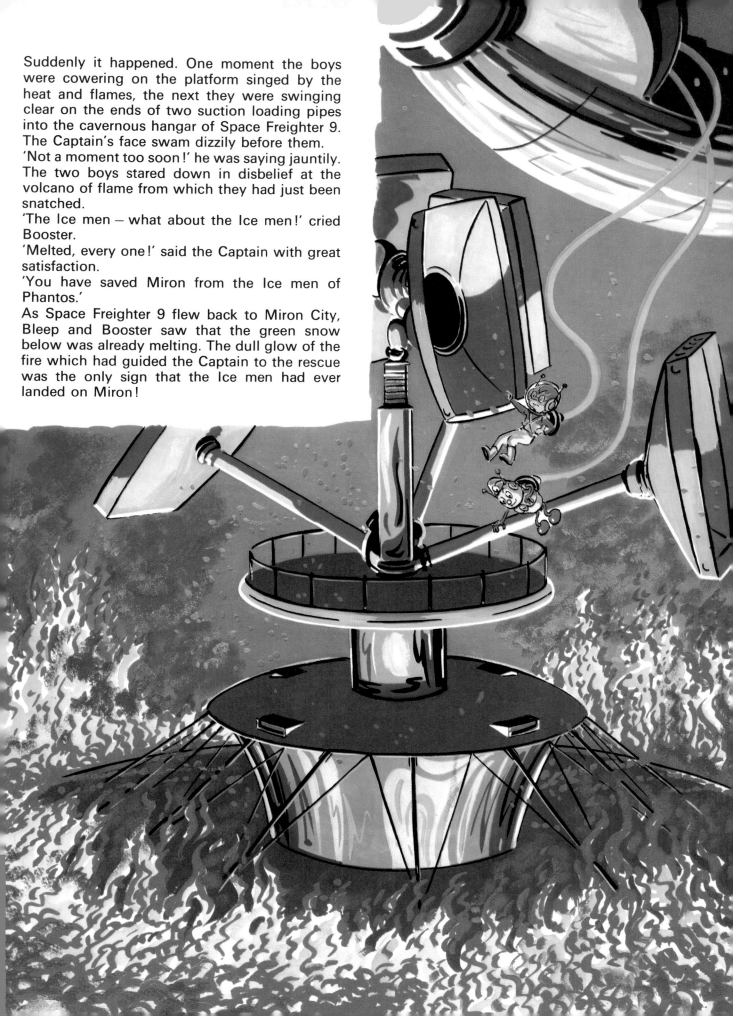

Suddenly it happened. One moment the boys were cowering on the platform singed by the heat and flames, the next they were swinging clear on the ends of two suction loading pipes into the cavernous hangar of Space Freighter 9. The Captain's face swam dizzily before them.

'Not a moment too soon!' he was saying jauntily. The two boys stared down in disbelief at the volcano of flame from which they had just been snatched.

'The Ice men — what about the Ice men!' cried Booster.

'Melted, every one!' said the Captain with great satisfaction.

'You have saved Miron from the Ice men of Phantos.'

As Space Freighter 9 flew back to Miron City, Bleep and Booster saw that the green snow below was already melting. The dull glow of the fire which had guided the Captain to the rescue was the only sign that the Ice men had ever landed on Miron!

Gemini X

John and Peter investigate the scorch marks on Gemini X's heat shield. This two-ton spacecraft orbited the earth 43 times and achieved the first fully successful link-up with an Agena satellite.

Scorched and blackened by the intense heat of re-entry into the atmosphere, Gemini X was brought all the way from America to the 'Blue Peter' studio! In this very spacecraft, Astronauts John W. Young and Michael Collins hurtled through space at over 17,000 miles an hour. They took part in a special series of tests that have taken space explorers a giant step forward on their journey to the moon. The next stages in the moon race are being taken by the three-man Apollo. On the opposite page you can see how the astronauts and their equipment are packed inside the biggest American spacecraft.

This scale model shows how cramped conditions were inside the two-man Gemini. The pilot can change the height and plane of its orbit by direct control.

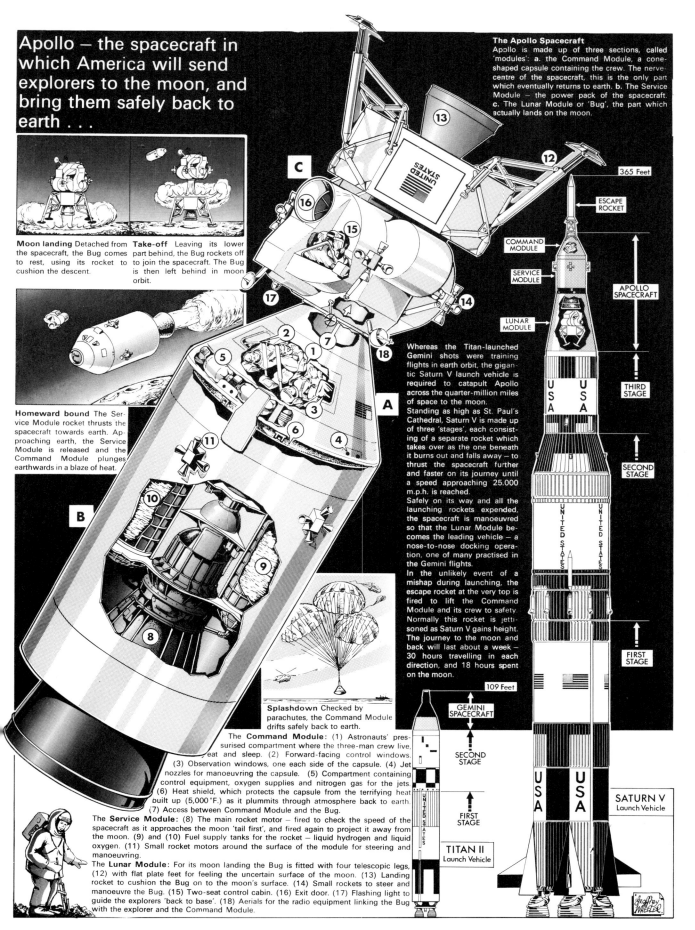

Apollo — the spacecraft in which America will send explorers to the moon, and bring them safely back to earth . . .

Moon landing Detached from the spacecraft, the Bug comes to rest, using its rocket to cushion the descent.

Take-off Leaving its lower part behind, the Bug rockets off to join the spacecraft. The Bug is then left behind in moon orbit.

Homeward bound The Service Module rocket thrusts the spacecraft towards earth. Approaching earth, the Service Module is released and the Command Module plunges earthwards in a blaze of heat.

The Apollo Spacecraft
Apollo is made up of three sections, called 'modules': **a.** the Command Module, a cone-shaped capsule containing the crew. The nerve-centre of the spacecraft, this is the only part which eventually returns to earth. **b.** The Service Module — the power pack of the spacecraft. **c.** The Lunar Module or 'Bug', the part which actually lands on the moon.

UNITED STATES

365 Feet

ESCAPE ROCKET

COMMAND MODULE

SERVICE MODULE

APOLLO SPACECRAFT

LUNAR MODULE

THIRD STAGE

SECOND STAGE

USA

FIRST STAGE

Whereas the Titan-launched Gemini shots were training flights in earth orbit, the gigantic Saturn V launch vehicle is required to catapult Apollo across the quarter-million miles of space to the moon.
Standing as high as St. Paul's Cathedral, Saturn V is made up of three 'stages', each consisting of a separate rocket which takes over as the one beneath it burns out and falls away — to thrust the spacecraft further and faster on its journey until a speed approaching 25,000 m.p.h. is reached.
Safely on its way and all the launching rockets expended, the spacecraft is manoeuvred so that the Lunar Module becomes the leading vehicle — a nose-to-nose docking operation, one of many practised in the Gemini flights.
In the unlikely event of a mishap during launching, the escape rocket at the very top is fired to lift the Command Module and its crew to safety. Normally this rocket is jettisoned as Saturn V gains height. The journey to the moon and back will last about a week — 30 hours travelling in each direction, and 18 hours spent on the moon.

109 Feet

GEMINI SPACECRAFT

SECOND STAGE

FIRST STAGE

UNITED STATES

TITAN II Launch Vehicle

USA

SATURN V Launch Vehicle

Splashdown Checked by parachutes, the Command Module drifts safely back to earth.

The **Command Module**: (1) Astronauts' pressurised compartment where the three-man crew live, eat and sleep. (2) Forward-facing control windows. (3) Observation windows, one each side of the capsule. (4) Jet nozzles for manoeuvring the capsule. (5) Compartment containing control equipment, oxygen supplies and nitrogen gas for the jets. (6) Heat shield, which protects the capsule from the terrifying heat built up (5,000°F.) as it plummits through atmosphere back to earth. (7) Access between Command Module and the Bug.
The **Service Module**: (8) The main rocket motor — fired to check the speed of the spacecraft as it approaches the moon 'tail first', and fired again to project it away from the moon. (9) and (10) Fuel supply tanks for the rocket — liquid hydrogen and liquid oxygen. (11) Small rocket motors around the surface of the module for steering and manoeuvring.
The **Lunar Module**: For its moon landing the Bug is fitted with four telescopic legs, (12) with flat plate feet for feeling the uncertain surface of the moon. (13) Landing rocket to cushion the Bug on to the moon's surface. (14) Small rockets to steer and manoeuvre the Bug. (15) Two-seat control cabin. (16) Exit door. (17) Flashing light to guide the explorers 'back to base'. (18) Aerials for the radio equipment linking the Bug with the explorer and the Command Module.

LIFE SAVING

I don't know if there's something special about Crystal Palace, but it was the place chosen for both John and me to make our first appearances on 'Blue Peter'.

Three years ago John went roaring down the artificial ski slope and fell flat on his face at the feet of the 'Blue Peter' cameraman.

Two years later, and about 200 yards from the same spot, I made my debut by jumping – with all my clothes on – into the swimming pool at the National Recreation Centre. I came to the surface and was promptly pushed under again by John. I had arrived on 'Blue Peter'.

I wanted to do something about life saving for my first programme, because it's something I've been very keen on ever since I took my Pre-liminary Safety Award when I was ten years old.

John was pushing me under, not because he thought it was his turn to speak and that was the best way to shut me up, but because we were showing what happens when a rescuer approaches a drowning man. I used to think that anyone drowning would be so grateful to his rescuer that he would do everything the rescuer asked. Not a bit of it! A drowning man is in a panic because he's fighting for his life. He'll grab the first thing that comes anywhere near him, and that's usually the arms or the hair of the poor chap who's trying to pull him out. Many a would-be rescuer has been drowned by the very man he's trying to save! The best thing to do is to stay out of reach until the drowning man has exhausted himself, then swim round him – going under water if necessary – and grab hold of him from behind. That way you'll not only be saving yourself from being pushed under, but you'll also be in the best position to keep the drowning man's head above water and to tow him to safety.

If you see someone drowning, the instinctive thing to do is to dive in and swim out to help him. But that, strangely enough, is the *last* thing you should do. There are plenty of other, safer things, to try first. Look around to see if there's anything to reach him with, like a pole or the branch of a tree, but always kneel or lie down when you're reaching out over the water so that you can stretch further, and stand less chance of being pulled

I have been keen on life saving ever since I took my Preliminary Safety Award when I was ten years old.

Always jump, never dive into unknown water. You never know what might be under the surface.

As soon as you're in the water, get rid of as many clothes as you can.

Never approach a drowning man from the front. He'll be in a panic and might push *you* under.

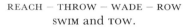

Keep a safe distance until he's exhausted himself – then dive under water . . .

. . . and come to the surface behind him.

in yourself. Throwing a rope would be ideal, but if there isn't one handy, throw anything that will float. If the drowning person can hold on to something, it will give him confidence, and stop him from exhausting himself by thrashing about in the water. It may sound silly, but try *wading* into the water before you think of diving – you may find that he's only just out of his depth and that you can reach him with a pole. Remember you are far more in command standing on your feet than you are when swimming. Don't forget to look around for a boat. Rowing is much faster than swimming, and you can be far more help in a boat than you can be in the water.

The Royal Life Saving Society sum this up in seven words:

REACH – THROW – WADE – ROW SWIM and TOW.

If there's nothing else for it but to swim, remember always to *jump* rather than dive into unknown water. You never know what hazards may lie beneath the surface. If you'd like to have a go at life saving, enquire at your local swimming baths; and if they can't help you, write to:

The Royal Life Saving Society,
14 Devonshire Street,
London, W.1.

They'll put you in touch with your nearest life saving Instructor.
John was very interested in everything I'd shown him, and after I'd towed him to the side of the baths, he said: 'I feel I've learnt so much, I wish someone would fall in and then I could try a rescue myself.'

There was a small cry of 'Help!' from the other side of the baths, and Val, neatly and suitably dressed in jeans and a tee shirt, stepped gracefully off the side of the baths into the warm blue water of the swimming pool.

John was across the pool like an arrow. He duck-dived under the water like a bronze medallist and came up to grab Val by the head in *nearly* the approved manner. It may have lacked style and grace – and Val was a little more cooperative than the average drowning person, but at least he got her back to the side with her head well above water.

Let's face it, the only criterion in life saving is that you get them out of the water – *alive*!

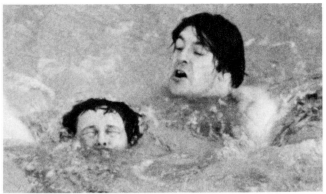

Now you're in the best position to grab him . . .

. . . and tow him away to safety.

John was hoping to find someone to rescue when there was a faint cry of 'help' from the other side of the baths.

A few firm strokes carried John round behind Val into the best position to make a rescue.

John's 'hold' may have lacked style, but at least he got Val safely to the side.

Peter demonstrates the 'two handed' tow.

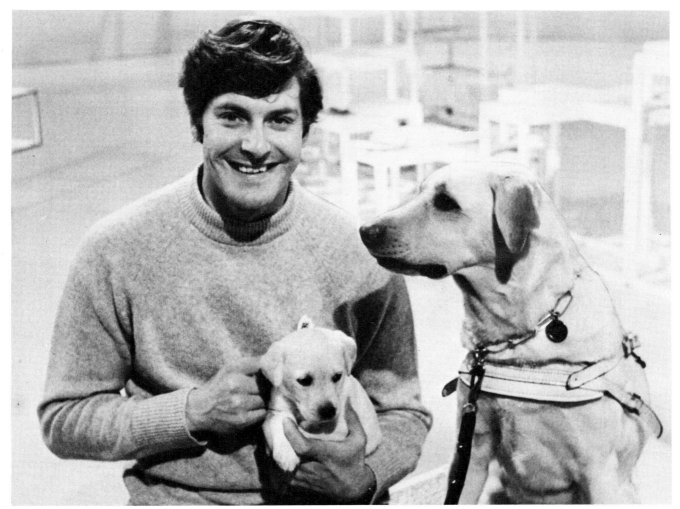

Our guide dog, Honey, passed her tests with flying colours. Will Cindy, her half sister, be as successful?

EYES FOR THE BLIND

Thanks to 'Blue Peter' viewers, a blind music teacher is able to carry on with her work, looked after by Honey, our 'Blue Peter' guide dog.

Now we're well on our way to helping another blind person with Cindy, our new trainee guide dog puppy. Honey was bought by 'Blue Peter' viewers who collected enough milk bottle tops to buy two and a half guide dogs. But before guide dogs start their intensive training they have to be 'puppy walked', which means that the puppy goes to live with a family, and is brought up like an ordinary well-trained dog until it's old enough to learn how to be a guide dog.

This was exactly what we did with Honey, but we've never really stopped missing her since the day she left.

So, as we still had enough silver paper in the kitty to pay for one and a half guide dogs' training – and as we happened to know that the Guide Dogs for

the Blind Association was desperate for puppy walkers, we decided to try again.

On April 4th, 1968, a litter of ten five-week-old yellow labradors arrived at the 'Blue Peter' studio. And with them came Derek Freeman, the Guide Dog for the Blind Puppy Walking Manager. After giving the puppies a thorough examination, Derek picked out Cindy.

'She's just the puppy for you,' he said. 'Strong and healthy and unafraid.'

We agreed, Cindy was adorable, and another thing we were pleased about was that she was Honey's half-sister. We thought that was a good omen – and so far we've been right. Cindy is getting on splendidly and we hope that by the time we write our next 'Blue Peter' Book, we'll be able to show you two fully trained pairs of eyes for the blind.

37

John as a waiter

The day I took 'Blue Peter' cameras behind the scenes at the London Hilton Hotel, I met a lot of interesting people. Some were never seen by the public – and even those smartly uniformed figures the hotel guests meet every day spend most of their lives behind mysterious doors marked 'Staff Only'. It was this *unseen* part that interested me most. Take Stamos, the waiter in the International Restaurant. Where did he learn to lay tables so deftly and efficiently? How did he know so much about wine and food? What exactly went on when he disappeared behind that swinging door?

To find the answer to these, and many other questions, I had to spend a day at the Westminster Technical College Hotel School in Vincent Square, London. French is the international language of top class catering, or, I should say, 'haute cuisine', so it's not surprising that trainee waiters have to have French lessons. Not only must a waiter understand the menu, which is always in French, and be able to explain to a customer exactly what each dish is, but he must also write the order in French and give any further instructions to the chef in French as well. Even if the waiter comes from Yorkshire and the

chef from Bermondsey, if the waiter gives the order in English, the chef will say something very rude back to him in French!

Personal hygiene is important. A waiter's hands must be scrupulously clean, his nails cut short, and his hair neat and tidy. His clothes must be smart and tidy, too. Students have to provide themselves with black shoes, dress trousers, white shirt and bow tie. Clip-on bow ties are not encouraged – there's always a danger they'll fall into the soup.

Laying a table is largely a matter of common sense. You start with the things for the first course on the

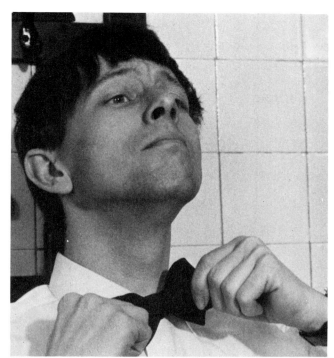
A waiter's bow tie must be hand tied. A clip on bow might fall in the soup.

All conversation must be in French. If a waiter speaks to a chef in English, he might get a rude reply – in French!

outside and gradually work your way in, so that the knife and fork for the main course end up nearest the plate. The dessert fork and spoon go above the plate, and the butter knife on the side plate, but parallel with the other cutlery – I lost marks for laying mine across the plate. I also lost marks for calling things by the wrong names. Would you know a pair of lobster crackers if you saw them? Or would you be fooled like I was, and think they were a giant-sized pair of nut crackers?

Part of the waiters course is devoted to the study of wine. In many restaurants there's a special waiter who does nothing else but serve drinks. He has to know all the hundreds of different kinds of wine. And he has to be able to advise customers which is the best wine to drink with which particular food. That's in addition to knowing the correct glass and right temperature for each particular wine, and how to pour without spilling one drop on the tablecloth. The answer to that's a deft twist as you take bottle from glass – and there's even a technique for opening the bottles. I had a go at opening a bottle of champagne. I got the little wire cage off all right, put both thumbs firmly under the cork, and – Bam! I managed to land the cork at least 30 yards from the bottle, but my instructor was not impressed. I should have wrapped a napkin round the top of the bottle and the cork should have remained in the napkin, instead of zooming across the room.

After a day at the Hotel School, I decided to put what I had learnt into practice, and where better to begin than the International Restaurant at the Hilton Hotel, with my friend Stamos to keep an eye on me. He fitted me out with a smart waiter's suit (he even insisted on parting my hair!) checked my table laying, and retired to a corner of the room whilst I waited, a little nervously, for my first real paying customers. I had been told that very famous people sometimes had lunch at the International Restaurant and Stamos had warned me not to stare

My champagne cork made a super noise, but the instructor was not impressed.

Peter and Val both ordered quite easy first courses — Val ordered hors d'oeuvres, and Peter smoked salmon — but for their main dish they ordered . . .

. . . Steak au poivre flambé, which is steak flamed with brandy — by the waiter!

at them or ask for autographs, but to treat them like ordinary people — as if they weren't famous at all. However, I didn't think I'd see anyone quite so famous as the people I saw walking towards my table. Or did I?

It was none other than V*L*R*E S*N*L*T*N and P*T*R P*R*E* from that well known programme B*U* P*T*R!

I showed them to a quiet table by the window, and of course, I had to pretend that I didn't know them, and they had to pretend they didn't know me. I folded Val's napkin over her lap in the approved manner. Peter very helpfully did his own, and I took the orders. Val ordered hors d'oeuvres for her first course and Peter smoked salmon. I served from the left, as I'd been taught, without dropping or spilling a single thing. So far, so good.

'And to follow, sir?'

'Steak au poivre flambé.'

'I'll have the same,' said Val, without batting an eyelid.

'Certainly, sir.'

You must be joking, I thought, as I wrote down the order and took it to the chef. Steak au poivre flambé is steak with pepper — and sauce flamed with brandy at the table — by the waiter! I hope the London Fire Brigade is standing by, that's all!

'Ça marche — deux steaks au poivre,' the chef's voice boomed, and the kitchen sprang into action. One under-chef started beating two pieces of steak to death with a mallet to make them tender, and whilst another was lovingly creating the sauce, the

first one placed the steaks on the griddle and watched them like a hawk.

Back in the restaurant I was pouring the wine for Val, and every drop went into the glass!

I returned to the kitchen to collect my order. I gave the table number in French (this chef was from Spain, not Bermondsey, but we still had to speak in French. I now understood why. In a trade that attracts men from all over Europe, a common language is essential). Then with my deux steaks au poivre about to be flambéd, I set off back to the table. I carefully put the steaks in a silver frying pan and lit my little charcoal grill. It's the amount of brandy you put on the steak that's the tricky bit — too little and nothing happens, too much and you've lost your eyebrows.

One, two, three — Go!

I let it have about half a cupful.

Woof! A satisfying blue flame leapt up from the pan.

'Gosh!' said Val.

But I kept my eyes firmly on the steak as I served it, taking care to get the spoon firmly *under* the meat as I'd been taught, and to put the sauce by the *side* of the steak.

'My steak's delicious. How's yours?' said Val.

'Very good,' said Peter.

'Thank you, sir,' I said, and I walked over to Stamos to ask him how I had fared as a waiter.

'Not bad for the first time,' he said. 'But next time you do a flambé at the table, try not to look as though you're firing a rocket at Cape Kennedy!'

40

Chocolate apples

We didn't have these apples at the Hilton Hotel — but they're delicious to eat and extremely simple to make. As well as using different kinds of chocolate — plain, white or caramel — you can have different decorations, too. I've used rice krispies, jelly sweets, raisins and liquorice allsorts. This is how you make them:

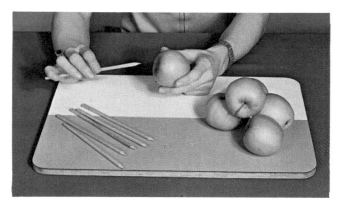

1 After washing and drying your apple, push a clean wooden skewer through the centre. You can also use thin dowelling.

2 Break the chocolate into pieces in a bowl. You'll find that the plain chocolate is the easiest to melt.

3 Melt the chocolate by standing the basin in a saucepan or larger basin that has some warm water in it. Stir until smooth and runny.

4 Dip the apple in the chocolate stirring it round to coat it well.

5 Next dip the apple in a bowl of rice krispies and put on greaseproof paper until the chocolate sets.

6 The creamy white type of chocolate looks good with small jelly sweets decorating it.

7 The caramel type of chocolate goes well with seedless raisins or you could use glacé cherries.

8 I made the clown's face from raisins and liquorice allsorts. You could also use chopped nuts, or desiccated coconut.

Val goes showjumping

'Grip tighter with your knees, Val.'

'Keep your hands down as she approaches the fence.'

Misty cantered smartly towards the biggest fence in the field. It was only three feet high, but at that moment it seemed as tall as a double decker bus. Suddenly we were airborne, and somehow I managed to stay in the saddle as we landed and cantered back to where Alan Oliver was standing.

'Not bad,' he said. 'In fact, for the first time – quite good!'

I had learned to ride when I was nine years old, but this was the very first time I'd ever taken a horse over a jump. Alan had learned to ride when he was four years old, and by the time he was nine, he'd won his first show jumping competition. Since then, he's won hundreds of competitions all over the world. Today, he was on Sweep – a horse he has ridden to victory in over thirty events.

He gave Sweep a fast canter round the meadow, whilst the jumps were raised to competition height. Alan had told me always to let the horse have a run round to settle him down before approaching the first jump. I sat on Misty and watched. Alan pulled the horse gently round until they were dead centre of the fence. A slight touch with the heels, Sweep bounded forward as if unleashed, and they soared over poles in a classically extended position. There was complete sympathy between horse and rider. As soon as Sweep had taken off, Alan's eyes were already on the next fence, because each landing is

I was lucky because my instructor was one of the world's greatest show jumpers – Alan Oliver.

Misty soared into the air and I was over my first jump.

Misty leapt higher than I bargained for and I ended up on the grass.

also part of the approach to the following jump. On intricate competition courses, it's sometimes necessary to turn the horse in the air before landing, so as to be in the best position for the next jump.

Alan completed his round flawlessly and brought Sweep back to where Misty and I were standing.

'I want you to go round again, Val, and this time I'm raising your fences six inches.'

'Are you sure . . .' I began.

'Remember to look up when you ride towards the

I listened carefully to Alan's instructions.

jump – and aim for the middle,' said Alan.

There didn't seem to be any room for argument, so I obediently trotted off on Misty as the course was prepared.

This time I felt a great deal better – in fact, I thought my turn into the spread was really quite professional. Misty leapt into the air, I felt one second of hesitation as I was in mid-flight, and then,

crash! I fell headlong into the grass, and riderless Misty cantered gaily towards the other end of the meadow.

Alan wasn't in the least upset.

'You get plenty of falls when you're jumping,' he said, as he helped me to my feet.

'Now you'd better get back on Misty and go round again.'

I must admit I felt a bit shaken up, but Alan was absolutely right to make me ride again straight away. I climbed back onto Misty, and this time I got round without a fault.

I was improving, but somehow I don't think I'll make the Horse of the Year Show *this* season.

Bengo by Tim

1 One morning, as Bengo passed the butcher's shop, the butcher called to him and gave him a beautiful bone.

2 Bengo was delighted. Carrying the bone he rushed home as fast as he could —

3 — and started to dig a big hole to bury it, in order to keep it for a special occasion.

4 But he was interrupted by barking. It came from the end of the garden. Perhaps another dog was after his bone, so Bengo went to investigate.

5 He crept towards the sound which came from behind the dustbin, and he was just about to pounce when a small head popped around the corner. It was a baby seal!

6 'Hello,' said Bengo, 'you must be from the Circus. Follow me and I'll take you home!' But the baby seal was far too frightened to say anything.

7 Suddenly it dashed from behind the bin — scuttled down the garden path —

8 — and dived into the goldfish pond.

9 Bengo was baffled! He sat by the side of the pond wondering what on earth he could do.

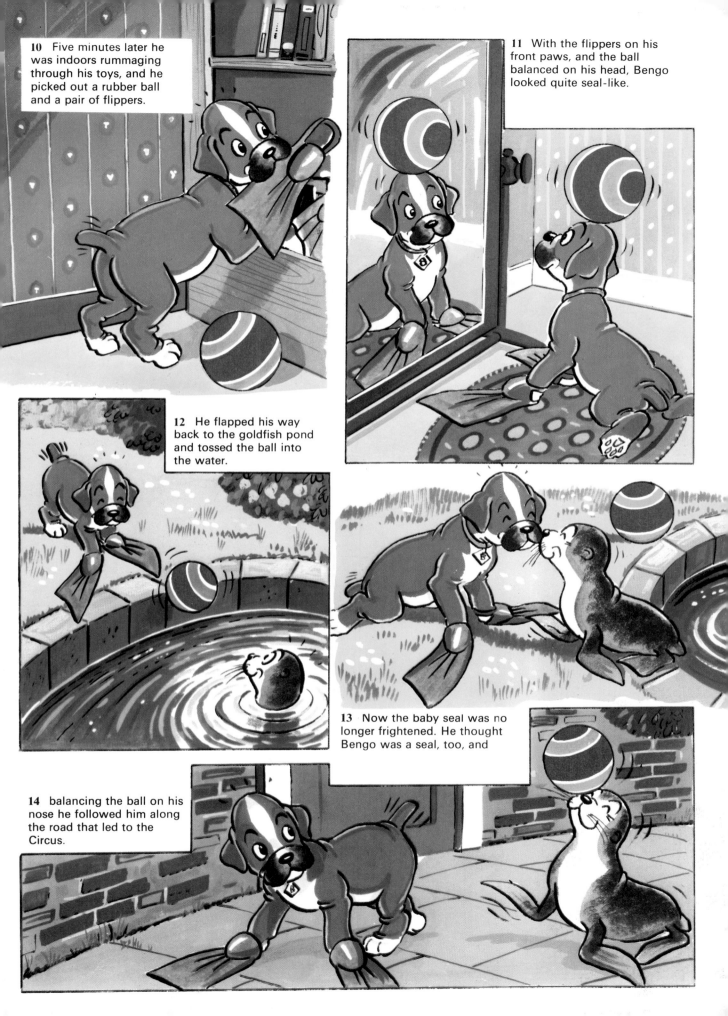

10 Five minutes later he was indoors rummaging through his toys, and he picked out a rubber ball and a pair of flippers.

11 With the flippers on his front paws, and the ball balanced on his head, Bengo looked quite seal-like.

12 He flapped his way back to the goldfish pond and tossed the ball into the water.

13 Now the baby seal was no longer frightened. He thought Bengo was a seal, too, and

14 balancing the ball on his nose he followed him along the road that led to the Circus.

CIRCUS

15 When they arrived, all the clowns ran out to welcome them.

16 The ringmaster appeared in his best top hat and patted Bengo on the head.

17 But the baby seal's mother was the most pleased of all and Bengo was given a very wet kiss for looking after her young one.

18 For a special treat he was allowed to join the seal act during the afternoon performance. And as the audience clapped and cheered, Bengo thought it was one of the best days of his life!

Petra's great grand puppies

Last year, when we showed you three generations of 'Blue Peter' dogs, we said that perhaps in this book we'd be able to show you four generations – Well, we were right!

Petra became a great-grandmother on 16th October 1967, when two puppies were born to Mandy, her granddaughter. They were both dog puppies, and we decided to call them Zebedee and Zabadak. By the time they were three months old their mischievousness had caused lots of trouble.

They always did their bad deeds together – things like dragging a newly washed sheet from a clothes line and burying it; and digging a hole in a fence – escaping through it into a nearby graveyard and chewing up a wreath. But now they're older, Zebedee and Zabadak are well behaved – a credit to their famous great-grandmother, Petra!

Zebedee and Zabadak with Petra, their great-grandmother, Mandy, their mother, and great-uncle Patch.

Here are the puppies when they were three months old. Zebedee, who has a much smoother coat than his brother, was nick-named Piggy because he was so greedy.

G

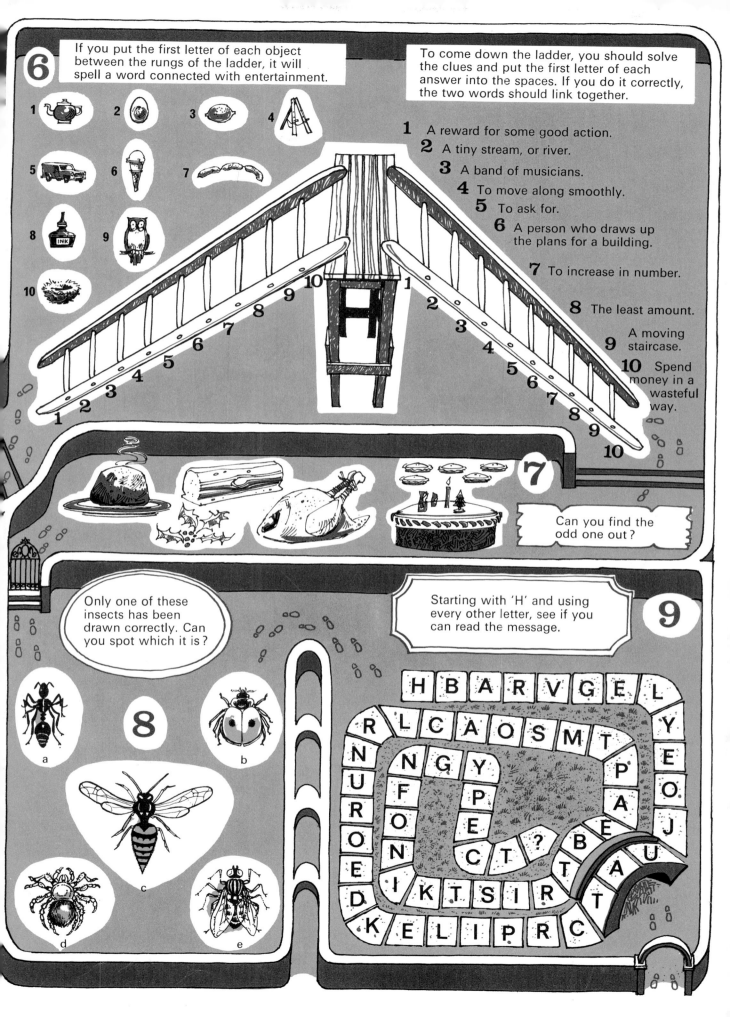

6 If you put the first letter of each object between the rungs of the ladder, it will spell a word connected with entertainment.

1 2 3 4 5 6 7 8 9 10

To come down the ladder, you should solve the clues and put the first letter of each answer into the spaces. If you do it correctly, the two words should link together.

1 A reward for some good action.
2 A tiny stream, or river.
3 A band of musicians.
4 To move along smoothly.
5 To ask for.
6 A person who draws up the plans for a building.
7 To increase in number.
8 The least amount.
9 A moving staircase.
10 Spend money in a wasteful way.

7 Can you find the odd one out?

Only one of these insects has been drawn correctly. Can you spot which it is?

8

a
b
c
d
e

9 Starting with 'H' and using every other letter, see if you can read the message.

H B A R V G E L
R L C A O S M T
N N G Y P
U F O P E
R O N E C T ?
O I K T S I R
E D K E L I P R C

TABLE TOP TANKS

Do you collect models of vintage vehicles? Here are some you can make for yourself. These are Mark IV tanks. They took part in the first major tank battle at Cambrai, in France, over fifty years ago. To make them, all you will need is cardboard, matchboxes and glue.

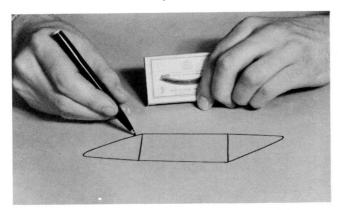

1 Start with the sides. Lay a large matchbox on a sheet of thin card and draw round it. Make a mark about two inches from each end of the box shape and draw in the curve for the front and back of the tank.

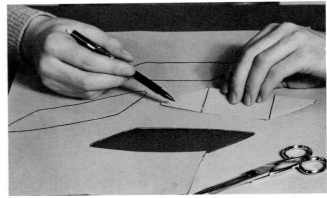

2 You will need four pieces of card exactly the same size. Cut out your first shape just inside the outline and use it as a pattern.

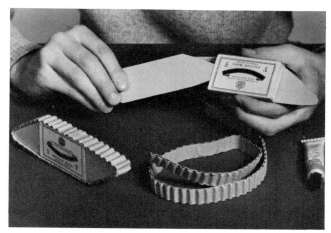

3 For each side slot two pieces of card through a large matchbox. Glue on a strip of corrugated card to make the caterpillar tracks.

4 You will need four small matchboxes to make the body of the tank. Cardboard ones are best. Take two of the boxes, push the trays out about $\frac{1}{2}$ inch, and slot them together. This makes the fuel tank. Two more boxes glued together and stuck on top complete the body.

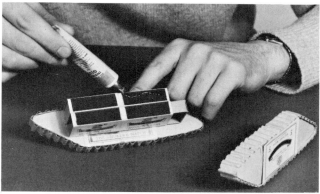

5 Glue the sides to the body. Remember to keep the body clear of the tracks and to put the fuel tank at the back.

6 Both side gun turrets are made from one large matchbox tray. Mark the tray as I have done. First cut the box in half then trim away the angles. Fill in the open side with a little piece of card.

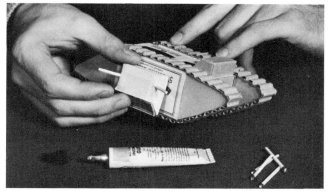

7 Stick one gun turret on each side of the Mark IV and add guns made from used matches. The top turret is made from half a small matchbox tray.

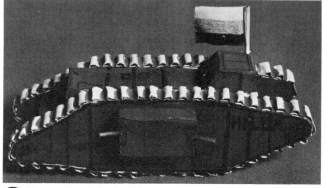

8 Paint the Mark IV green and add details with a black pen. I have made Hilda, the famous tank that led the battle of Cambrai. You can make a layout with a tray of earth or sand and some twigs.

A story by Michael Bond illustrated by Peggy Fortnum

Paddington to the rescue

Paddington peered round the Browns' breakfast table, a large portion of bacon and eggs poised halfway to his mouth, and stared at the rest of the family in amazement.

'We're all going to the *seaside*, Mr Brown?' he exclaimed, looking as if he could hardly believe his ears. 'In *November*?'

'There's a first time for everything,' said Mr Brown vaguely. 'Besides, it'll set us up for the winter. A breath of sea air will do us the world of good.'

Mrs Brown gave one of her 'let's change the subject' looks. 'I should have a good breakfast,' she broke in. 'We've a long journey ahead of us and you ought to fill in all the odd corners.'

'Anyone who's prepared to cook enough bacon and eggs to fill in all that bear's corners is welcome,' said Mrs Bird meaningly.

The Browns' housekeeper paused at the dining-room door and looked back at the table. 'And if certain people don't buck their ideas up, they're liable to find themselves left behind.'

A look of alarm came over Paddington's face, and for the next few moments the sound of toast being crunched at high speed echoed round the room as he busied himself with his marmalade jar.

However, shortly afterwards he disappeared upstairs, and after giving his whiskers a quick going-over with the flannel, he turned his attention to the all-important matter of what to take with him.

Paddington had a hopeful nature and even though the barometer in the hall had been stuck at wet and windy for over a week, it was difficult not to associate the seaside with fun and games on the beach, so that by the time he made his way back down again he was pretty heavily laden.

'I hope they're all games for one person,' said Mrs

Bird grimly, when she bumped into him halfway down the stairs. 'Judging by the look of the weather, you'll have the beach to yourself!'

Paddington looked most upset as he followed Mrs Bird's gaze out of the landing window, for apart from a bucket and spade and an inflatable rubber raft, he'd managed to collect several beach balls, a tennis racket, a fishing net, a large tyre which hung round his neck like an oversize collar, not to mention a straw hat which he'd perched precariously on top of his usual felt one; all of which seemed somewhat out of place against the leaden sky overhead.

'Never mind,' said Judy, as she helped disentangle the bucket and spade from the pile. 'We should never have got it all in the taxi.'

'The *taxi*?' echoed Paddington, nearly falling the rest of the way downstairs in his surprise. 'I've never heard of anyone going to the seaside in a taxi before!'

'It's only taking us as far as the station,' explained Jonathan. 'Dad's booked seats on the train.'

Paddington began to look more and more mystified as he absorbed this latest piece of information. The Browns often had days out at the sea, but almost always they were very haphazard 'on the spur of the moment' affairs, whereas this one seemed particularly well organised. In fact, if he'd had more time to consider the matter, it might have struck him as very odd indeed.

But Paddington wasn't the sort of bear to query his good fortune, and by the time they reached the station his feeling of surprise had long since given way to one of excitement.

It wasn't often he had the chance to ride on a train, and he grew even more excited as he settled back in his seat and rubbed a hole on the patch of steam on the window in order to peer out at the countryside flashing past outside. And when, some while later, Mr Brown looked at his watch and announced that they would all be having lunch in the dining-car, his excitement practically reached fever pitch.

'I've never been in a dining-room on wheels before, Mr Brown,' he exclaimed.

'Perhaps you'd like to go along and see if there are any vacant seats,' said Mr Brown generously.

Paddington needed no second bidding, and Mrs Brown looked at her husband nervously as there was a flurry of duffle-coat and the door to the corridor slid shut. 'Do you think that was wise, Henry?' she asked.

'It's an important occasion,' said Mr Brown. 'We may as well let him make the most of it. Besides, if I know Paddington, he won't stray very far if there's any food about.'

For once Mr Brown was nearer the truth than even he imagined.

Having discovered that the dining-car itself was crowded, Paddington was about to leave when he sniffed the air several times and then turned his attention to a small hatch near the entrance. There were several interesting smells coming from the other side, and by standing on tip-toe he was just able to peer over the top.

As he did so his eyes grew round with astonishment, for he found himself looking into a different world. A world of hustle and bustle, of clanging pots and steam and sizzling pans, and a chef in a white coat doing a balancing act with a pile of plates as the train rocked on its way. There were several other people hard at work, and even as he watched, a waiter came dashing through a nearby door and deposited a pile of empty soup plates in the sink.

The chef looked up. 'Don't take any more orders for the fish,' he shouted. 'It's off!'

The waiter mopped his brow. 'I'm not surprised,' he retorted gloomily. 'Everybody's been asking for it this morning. It's one of them days. That's the way it goes. Some days it's meat. Some days it's fish.'

'Good job I stepped on it,' agreed the chef, stirring the contents of a large saucepan. 'Otherwise some of 'em would 'ave been unlucky.'

Paddington's eyes grew larger and larger as he listened to the conversation. He lowered himself down from the serving hatch with a thoughtful

expression on his face, and then made his way slowly along to the dining-room itself, placing his bucket and spade on a nearby rack for safety, before settling himself on the one remaining seat at a table near the door.

As he looked round the table the thoughtful expression suddenly gave way to one of alarm.

'I shouldn't eat that if I were you,' he announced,

addressing the man opposite in a loud stage-whisper. 'I think it's off!'

'*Off*?' The man paused, his mouth half open. 'It doesn't smell too bad,' he began doubtfully, applying his nose to the end of the fork. 'At least . . .' He took another sniff.

Paddington looked over his shoulder. 'I heard the chef tell one of the waiters,' he continued, knowledgeably. 'He said he'd stepped on it!'

The man opposite lowered his fork and looked distastefully at the remains of his lunch. 'I expect he only wanted to make it go further,' said Paddington comfortingly. 'They've had a rush on it.'

'Really!' snorted a lady in a fur coat at the next table. She pushed her plate to one side. 'I couldn't help overhearing . . . and I'm glad I did!'

Her husband nodded his agreement. 'I shouldn't eat too much of *that* if I were you,' he said, addressing a man farther down the aisle. 'The young bear gentleman with the bucket and spade saw the chef standing on it!'

In a matter of moments the dining-car was in an uproar.

'Actually jumped up and down on it, so I'm told,' announced a loud voice at the other end. 'It's a wonder we haven't all been poisoned.'

A man with a large walrus moustache took up the story. 'Ground it in with his heel,' he snorted. 'I've a jolly good mind to . . .'

Whatever else he'd been about to say or do was lost beneath a clinking of crockery and cries of 'waiter' as from all sides people began calling for their bills and making their way out of the dining-car, some of them looking very green indeed.

*   *   *   *

'I must say eating on a train is very pleasant,' said Mr Brown, some while later. He glanced round at the row of empty tables. 'I wonder more people don't do it. It's funny we should have it all to ourselves.'

The strange affair of the empty dining-car was a topic of conversation with the Browns for the rest of the journey.

Only Mrs Bird failed to join in. Not because she hadn't enjoyed her lunch, but because her eagle eyes had caught some very odd looks being cast in Paddington's direction by the staff – looks which not even a generous tip by Mr Brown entirely erased. However, it was a very gay party of Browns who finally alighted from the train and made their way down the long hill towards the sea. Paddington in particular grew more and more excited at the prospect and he hurried on ahead of the others waving his spade eagerly in the air.

But as they reached the promenade, even his enthusiasm began to die away. A chill east wind was

blowing and apart from a small group of figures who appeared to be erecting some kind of decorated stand near the pier, there wasn't a soul in sight.

After testing the water he hurriedly withdrew his paw and turned his attention to the important task of making a sandcastle. But a moment or two's digging in the cold, wet sand soon made even this pall.

Paddington stood up and surveyed his surroundings. 'Perhaps I could go on the pier, Mrs Brown?' he asked hopefully.

Mrs Brown looked at him doubtfully. 'I suppose he can't come to any harm, Henry,' she said, turning to her husband. 'I'd really like to take Jonathan and Judy shopping before they go back to school. They can go on afterwards if they want to.'

'But mind you're back here by three o'clock sharp,' she called out, as Paddington hurried off up the promenade. 'We've something very important arranged.'

Normally Mrs Brown's words would have given

Paddington food for thought, but with one and sixpence a week bun money burning a hole in his duffle-coat pocket they fell on largely deaf ears, for he didn't want to go back home again without having a go on *something* – even if it was only a chocolate machine.

The man at the turnstile eyed him gloomily as he took his sixpence. 'You won't find much open at this time of the year,' he warned, 'so don't come asking for yer money back.'

Thanking the man for his information, Paddington pushed his way through the turnstile and then hurried up the pier. A cold wind was blowing between the gaps in the boards and he was glad when at long last he reached the end. Looking around, he began to see what the man had meant and he rather wished he'd mentioned it before taking his sixpence instead of afterwards. The large amusement arcade which occupied most of the space, stood silent and shuttered, while the kiosks surrounding it were equally dark and deserted.

It was all most disappointing and he was about to turn and retrace his steps when he suddenly caught sight of an interesting looking machine standing in the shelter of a nearby doorway.

There was a picture of a large hand on the front, and beneath this were the words HAVE YOUR FORTUNE TOLD – ELECTRONICALLY!

Below this there was a picture of a man inserting sixpence into a slot while placing his other hand on a large metal plate containing, so the wording underneath explained, 'a thousand sensitive probes to read into your future'.

Paddington wasn't at all sure what a probe was, but he read the instructions carefully several times and even though there didn't seem to be a position on the control lever marked 'bears' he decided it looked very good value.

In the event however, it was somewhat disappointing. Far from there being a 'thousand sensitive probes' he could only count twenty-two, and most of these were so rusty they stuck halfway. For a few seconds the machine emitted a loud grinding noise and then, after a series of whirrs and clanks, a small piece of green cardboard fluttered into an opening near the base.

Paddington held the piece of card up to the light and as he did so he began to look more and more upset, for apart from the uninspiring news that his lucky colour for the day was 'blue', most of the space seemed to be taken up by the information that he was about to meet a dark lady bearing good tidings. Looking around the deserted pier he couldn't see a lady of any sort, let alone a dark one bearing tidings, and he was just about to throw the card away in disgust when his eye caught some wording near the bottom.

He peered at it with interest for a moment or two, and then, clutching the card firmly in his paw, hurried back down the pier with a determined expression on his face.

The man in charge of the entrance didn't seem best pleased at being disturbed a second time, and he looked even less pleased when Paddington explained the reason.

'You're coming into some money?' he repeated, reading the words on the bottom of the card. 'What's that got to do with me?'

Paddington held out his paw. 'I'd like to come into it now, please,' he announced.

The man stared at Paddington as if he could hardly believe his eyes, let alone his ears. ''ave you woken me up just to tell me that?' he demanded.

Paddington nodded. 'I've only got sixpence left,' he explained.

The man took a deep breath. 'If you go back up to the end of the pier,' he said sarcastically, 'you'll see a telescope. If I were you I'd bung it in there, 'cause that's what you'll need if you're going to find any money round 'ere.'

Paddington gave the door to the cubby-hole a hard stare as it slammed shut in his face, then he turned and retraced his steps slowly back up the pier again in the direction of the telescope.

Putting his last remaining sixpence in the slot, he clambered up onto the stand and applied his eye hopefully to the end.

At first everything seemed rather grey and misty, but then, as he waved it around, it began to get more interesting. All at once the horizon came into view, seemingly only a few yards away, and some of the waves against the skyline looked very choppy indeed.

Suddenly, Paddington glued his eye still more tightly against the eyepiece and then he nearly fell backwards off the platform in surprise. In the middle of the lens, as large as life, a small boat had appeared. But it wasn't so much the boat, or the way it was being tossed up and down, which caused his anxiety. It was the sight of a man standing up in the bows waving his arms in a most alarming way, and even as he watched, a loud cry of 'Help!' reached his ears.

Paddington looked wildly about but there wasn't a soul in sight. The only sign of life came from the spot on the promenade where the workmen had been erecting the stand. For some reason or other, quite a crowd seemed to have collected around it and Paddington tried waving his paws in the air, echoing the cry of 'Help' from the man in the boat, but he was much too far away for it to do any good.

Without pausing to consider the matter any further, he hurried across the pier and made his way down a flight of iron steps. Paddington was a brave bear at heart and it never crossed his mind to do other than

go to the aid of the man in distress, but after a few moments in the icy water, even he began to have second thoughts.

Apart from the fact that swimming wasn't one of his strong points, his duffle coat began to get heavier and heavier as it became waterlogged, and what with that and trying to keep his hat on with whichever paw happened to be out of the water, he soon realised that the chances of reaching the boat, let alone rescue the occupant, were very remote indeed.

A moment or so later a second cry of 'Help!' broke the afternoon air. For as he turned and tried to struggle back to the safety of the pier, Paddington suddenly had a nasty feeling that even this might be beyond him.

It was when he was going under for what seemed like the fiftieth time, and his struggles were growing weaker with every passing moment, that Paddington gradually became aware of a loud roaring noise in his ears.

Seconds later, though by now it all seemed part of an out-of-focus kind of dream, he heard voices, and almost at once felt himself being pulled bodily out of the water.

When Paddington came round, he found to his surprise that he was lying on his back surrounded by a large crowd of spectators, while a man in oilskins pulled his two front paws backwards and forwards. 'You've swallowed enough water to float a battleship,' explained a voice as he opened his eyes. 'Nothing to worry about, though – we're just giving you artificial respiration.'

Paddington sat up. '*Artificial* respiration?' he exclaimed in alarm. Although he'd spent his last sixpence, he felt sure Mr Brown would be only too pleased to pay for the real thing if only he could be found, and he gave the man a hard stare.

At the side of the crowd Mrs Brown heaved a sigh of relief. 'Thank goodness!' she said. 'He's himself again.'

'It'd take more than a pint or two of sea-water to sink Paddington,' said Mrs Bird firmly. But even she had suspiciously red-rimmed eyes.

'What I can't understand,' said Mr Brown, 'is what you were doing in the water in the first place.'

'I think I can,' said the man in oilskins. 'He heard me crying for help.'

He turned back to Paddington. 'I wasn't really in trouble,' he continued. 'It was all part of a demonstration.'

'A *demonstration*!' exclaimed Paddington hotly. He stared from one to the other of the faces in the crowd, and as he did so his eyes suddenly grew wider still, for at that moment three more familiar figures pushed their way forward.

'We're celebrating the anniversary of the launching of a new 'Blue Peter' Inshore Rescue Boat,' said Val, helping Paddington to his feet.

'As you looked after Joey so well last year,' added John, taking his other paw, 'we thought you'd like to come along as a special treat.'

'The rescue was meant to be part of the demonstration,' broke in Peter. 'We didn't dream we would have to rescue you instead.'

The man in the oilskins stood up. 'Fourteen people and a dog we've rescued so far,' he announced to the crowd. 'But this is the first time we've ever had to rescue a bear.'

'It must have taken quite a bit of courage to jump into that water,' he added, above the applause. 'I don't know as I should have fancied it.'

'I think you deserve a reward,' broke in Valerie.

'Speech!' cried someone at the back of the crowd. Paddington reached up in order to raise his hat to the assembly. 'I don't know that I *fancied* it,' he began simply. 'There didn't seem to be anything else to . . .' His voice trailed away and a strange look came over his face as he began groping on top of his head.

Mrs Brown clutched her husband's arm. 'Henry,' she said anxiously. 'You don't think he's having a relapse do you?'

'Crikey!' said Jonathan suddenly. 'It's not a relapse . . . it's his hat. It's missing!'

'Quick!' shouted the man in charge of the lifeboat as the matter was explained to him. 'Jump in.' He led Paddington across to the waiting craft and a moment later they disappeared out to sea in a flurry of white spray.

A sigh of relief went up a moment or so later as the boat turned and headed back towards the shore, more slowly this time, with Paddington standing up in the bows waving a familiar object in his paw.

'Thank goodness for that,' said Mrs Brown. 'We should never have heard the last of it otherwise.'

'What are you writing?' asked John, as Valerie took out a notebook.

'Fourteen people,' said Valerie. 'One dog, one bear . . . and one bear's hat!'

'Not a bad record when you come to think of it,' laughed Peter. 'Not a bad record at all.'

To that remark everyone present gave their whole-hearted agreement. And Paddington, as he stepped out of the Blue Peter Rescue Boat clutching a very bedraggled looking hat, agreed most of all.

Inside the lining he'd just come across the card bearing his fortune, and the more he considered the matter the more impressed he became. For not only had he met a dark lady bearing the good tidings of a reward, but blue had most certainly been his lucky colour for that particular day.

THE WIDEST THE HIGHEST THE GREATEST!

The story of Isambard Kingdom Brunel

A tunnel almost forty feet wide running under the River Thames – bridges more than a hundred feet high – a railway over a hundred miles long built through solid rock – the biggest ships that had ever put to sea!

And behind all these marvels – the greatest engineer the world has ever known – Isambard Kingdom Brunel!

His mother had been called Sophia Kingdom; his father, a Frenchman settled in England, was named Marc Isambard Brunel – that explains the name. The father was an engineer and contractor, and when his son was seventeen, he took him into his business – and that explains the tremendous interest and excitement Brunel felt all his life at the challenge of building and construction.

The firm was working on a new and daring project. London was growing – and so was London's traffic. In 1823 there was no bridge over the River Thames below London Bridge, and every day at Rother-hythe, four thousand people had to cross the river by a slow ferry. So a tunnel had been ordered, wide enough to take two streams of traffic and running right under the waters of the river itself.

For a year Brunel worked alongside his father, examining the site, testing the river bed, drawing plans and diagrams. At last work could start – and suddenly his father fell ill. Brunel had to take charge – he was just nineteen! He worked desperately hard – he was at the site sometimes for eighteen or twenty hours a day. He supervised everything.

First, a shaft was sunk down into the earth below the river, and from that point a shield was moved forward – an enormous iron structure, behind which thirty-six men could work. As they removed the earth and cleared it away behind them, the shield could be advanced, inch by laborious inch, and the tunnel bricked up and made safe behind them. It was desperately slow – in the first six months the tunnel grew only 100 feet – but it grew! There were many delays and dangers, but in November of 1827, young Isambard Kingdom Brunel presided over a dinner for forty guests and one hundred workmen. It was held in the tunnel itself – lit by gas and hung with crimson velvet, with the band of the Coldstream Guards playing!

Now it was certain that the tunnel would be finished, and Brunel looked round for a new adventure.

He found it in Bristol. Wealthy townspeople had announced a bridge building competition – they wanted a bridge to cross the deep gorge of the River Avon. Brunel was nearly twenty-five years old now – he was determined to have a go, and out of the hundreds of designs that were entered, the committee chose his to be the winner.

His bridge was called the Clifton Suspension Bridge. It stands there to this day – just as Brunel dreamed of it.

But now a new age was opening for England – the Railways were spreading across the country, and Bristol wanted a railway with trains running to and from London, 114 miles away. Brunel was asked to be chief engineer, and in 1833, the idea of the Great

The Thames tunnel.

Clifton suspension bridge.

Paddington station.

The Great Eastern.

The famous Tamar suspension bridge – Brunel's
last design. This year it is to be re-strengthened
to carry 3,000 ton freight trains.

Western Railway was born.

This was to be Brunel's greatest work. Right from
the start he surveyed every inch of the countryside
and decided where the track should run. He built
bridges – brick bridges, stone bridges, iron bridges –
he graded inclines and excavated tunnels.

On the Chippenham–Bath section of the line, he
planned his longest tunnel – the railway line would
drive right into the hillside for a stretch of nearly
two miles. It would be cut right through the rock
itself, without any supporting brickwork.

Box Tunnel employed 4,000 men and 300 horses. A
ton of candles was used every week for lighting
while it was being cut. At last it was finished, and
became another of Brunel's great triumphs.

He designed the great London station of Paddington
for his railway, and you can still see the huge iron
arches and glass roof exactly as planned by Brunel.
From beginning to end, from Paddington Station to
Bristol, the Great Western Railway was Brunel's
work.

But his imagination stretched beyond his railway.
Beyond Bristol lay the Atlantic, and beyond that –
America! There must be a great ship – a steam ship –
that would cross the Atlantic. In those days no such
ship existed, so Brunel decided to invent one.

He called his ship the *Great Western*, and again he
was a pioneer. She was successfully launched in
1837 – a ship of 1,340 tons with engines of 400 horse
power – and for years she was used regularly on the
Atlantic crossing.

Twenty years after the launching of the *Great
Western* came Brunel's last ship – the *Great Eastern*.
He was always ahead of his time, but with this last
ship he went almost too far.

The *Great Eastern* – 32,000 tons, 692 feet long, with
five funnels and six masts, 56-foot paddle-wheels
and a 24-foot screw propeller, was fantastic – a
creation only Brunel could have dreamed of.

Work on her started in 1852 – it was 1858 before she
was launched, after countless difficulties and set-
backs. A man was killed at her launching; and there
were disasters throughout her life at sea, but the
lessons other designers learnt from Brunel's sea-
going monster was to take British ship-building
right forward into the future.

Before he died, Brunel designed his last bridge. On
the borders of Devon and Cornwall, it stood 100
feet high above the tidal waters of the River Tamar.
Two graceful arches carried the track over a central
pillar – and a gentle incline led up to the bridge
itself, which stretched for more than 2,000 feet.
The Tamar Bridge was Brunel's masterpiece.

He died in 1859 – the year the Bridge was opened.
On one great arch was clearly carved the name of
the designer – I. K. BRUNEL – ENGINEER – 1859.
That is how he will always be remembered.

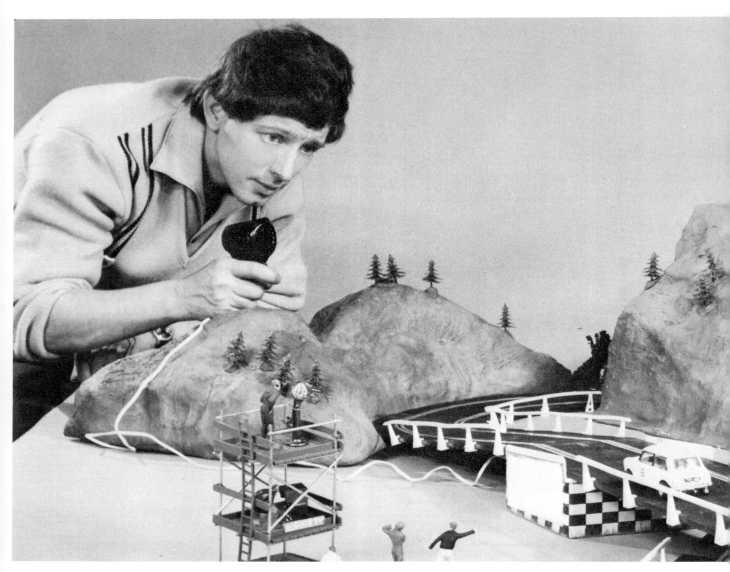

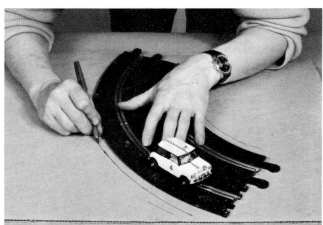

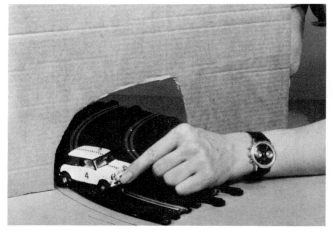

1 To make a mountain tunnel, start by marking the curve of the track on a thick cardboard base. The car may slew off on the turn, so allow room for this on either side of the track.

2 Cut out one end of the tunnel from another piece of cardboard. Grocers boxes are a good thickness. Make sure to leave plenty of headroom for the car. You will need two of these pieces — one for each end of the tunnel.

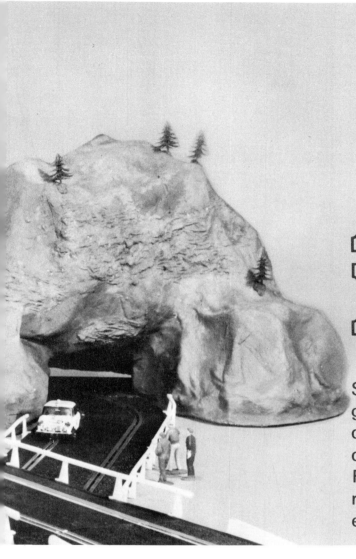

ALPINE RALLY

Slot car racing is fun, but if you're a good driver why not make your course a real test of your skill? I've converted my track into an Alpine Rally route. The thrills of mountain roads and tunnels make driving even more exciting!

3 Trim the ends of the tunnel roughly and use the pieces you have cut off to make the sides. It doesn't matter what shape the pieces are so long as the entrances to the tunnel leave enough room for the track and the cars. Fix the pieces firmly together and to the base with sticky tape.

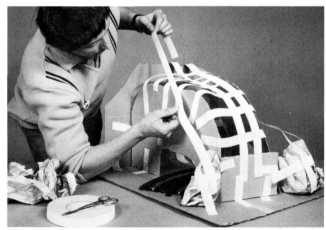

4 Cover the whole frame with strips of sticky tape. To get the real mountain look your tunnel shouldn't be too regular in shape. Screw up some newspaper to make the basis for mountain peaks and rocky outcrops.

5 To cover the framework, I've used plaster-covered bandage that is meant for broken legs! You can get this at chemists, or cut up into short lengths at model shops. Soak the plaster in water for a few seconds, squeeze it out and it's ready for use. This is a messy business, so put some newspaper down before you start.

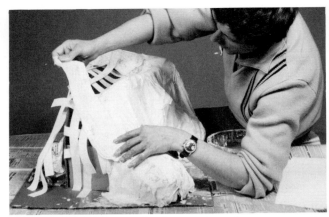

6 Lay the strips of plaster bandage over the frame. You can mould the rocky shape by adding more layers. If you don't want to use the plaster strips, you can cover the frame with papier maché — newspaper soaked in paste.

7 If you want trees on your mountain slopes, put them in place while the plaster is wet. It dries rock **hard**, so once the **plaster's dry**, it's very difficult to get the trees in.

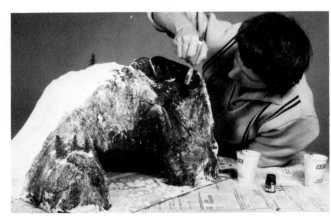

8 The plaster takes about an hour to dry. Once it's set you can start painting, but if you want a snowscape, leave it as it is!

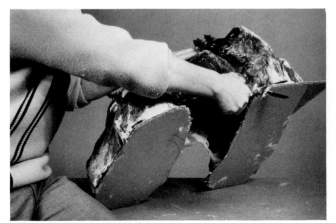

9 When the paint is dry, it's quite easy to cut away the cardboard base so that the tunnel can fit neatly over the track.

10 Using this method you can make very realistic landscapes for any layout. Why not make some for your railway, too?

Father David's deer

These Chinese deer are very special. They belong to the Duke of Bedford and live in Woburn Park. But how did they come to Europe? It's a strange story and it's thanks to one man these deer are alive today. Without his help, the whole species might have become extinct, and in his honour they are named after him.

1 A hundred years ago, Father David was a Missionary in China. In his spare time, he studied natural history, and

2 with only one guide, he would set out on lonely scientific expeditions.

3 In Paris, scientists were delighted with the wonderful rocks and plants he sent them, and

4 when the flowers bloomed, people had never seen anything like them.

5 Father David sent skins and feathers of strange animals and birds, too, but most of all

6 he wanted people to see the animals alive.

7 He persuaded a French Sea Captain to take some animals to Paris, hoping that they would survive the long journey.

8 The animals did arrive safely, and among them was the very first Giant Panda in Europe. But even more rare were

9 the Emperor of China's special deer. Only in China could these deer be found.

10 Father David pleaded with officials, and at last they agreed to give him just two of the special deer.

11 He packed the deer carefully in crates and sent them home to France.

12 In the Emperor's park, the deer grew fewer and fewer. Soon they died out altogether.

13 But in Paris, the two deer survived and soon there were many baby deer.

14 Thanks to Father David, a whole species have survived, and they were called Father David's deer in honour of the man who saved them.

15 Today you can see these deer in parks and zoos all over Britain, and all of them are descendants of the two deer that Father David sent from China, a hundred years ago.

The Tower of London

The Tower of London was built by William the Conqueror to protect and control the City of London. It has been used for nearly 900 years as a fortress — a palace — a treasure house — a prison — and a place of execution.

Nowadays, the only way to enter the tower is on foot by the drawbridge on Great Tower Hill. But once there was a river entrance, and it must have struck terror into the hearts of men and women who were brought there in Tudor times. In those days the river was lower and there was a landing stage, and it was there that traitors were landed – or those who the sovereign thought might be a threat to the throne.

The prisoners were taken up the steps and through a great gate which became known as 'Traitors'

This is Traitors' Gate. Persons who passed through here seldom left the tower alive.

Tower Green looks so peaceful in the sunshine, it is hard to believe it was once a place of bloody execution.

Only top people were executed on Tower Green – this death roll is impressive.

Gate'. As the gaolers slammed this sinister gate behind them, the prisoners knew they would never leave the tower alive.

But one person who *did* live to tell the tale was Queen Elizabeth I. She entered the gate twice. Once as a princess when she was imprisoned for six weeks, and once as a Queen when she insisted on passing through the gate.

Lady Jane Grey was seventeen when she was proclaimed Queen of England. Her reign lasted for only nine days.

'What was good enough for Elizabeth the Princess is good enough for Elizabeth the Queen,' she is reputed to have said.

Tower Green looks so gentle and beautiful today, it is impossible to believe that it was once the scene of bloody executions.

Only the very best people were executed on Tower Green. The rabble – the common criminals – the people of little account – met their deaths beyond the wall on Tower Hill. But the top people whose execution might have caused a riot or revolution, were quietly put to death on Tower Green. The

She was sentenced to death and taken to the Yeoman Gaoler's house to await execution.

These letters were carved on the walls of a cell in nearby Beauchamp Tower — where her husband also awaited execution.

death roll is impressive.
Queen Anne Boleyn
Margaret, Countess of Salisbury
Queen Catherine Howard
Jane, Viscountess of Rochford
Lady Jane Grey
Lady Jane Grey's story is probably the saddest of them all. She was 17 years old and had harmed no one. But she was a cousin of King Edward VI, and when he died, her ambitious father-in-law declared

There is an ancient superstition that if the ravens ever leave the tower, both Tower and Empire will collapse.

Today it is Yeoman Quartermaster Henry Johns' special responsibility to look after the ravens.

her Queen of England.
On June 10th, 1553, she was received in state at the Tower. Heralds proclaimed her accession from the four corners of the fortress. She was clad in Royal Robes and presented with the Crown Jewels.
But there was an uprising by Queen Mary who had a stronger claim to the throne. Mary was successful and Jane was declared a usurper and sentenced to death. She had been Queen for only nine days when she was taken to the Yeoman Gaoler's house to await her execution. She was married and her husband was imprisoned close by in Beauchamp Tower. To this day you can see carved on the wall the letters J.A.N.E. – probably by the hand of her sad young husband.
From her window overlooking the green, Jane saw the guards take her husband to be executed on Tower Hill and later watched them return with his

headless body. At the same time she could hear the carpenters driving home the nails as her *own* scaffold was erected.

Later that day, the guards came to take her – and with her ladies-in-waiting, she walked proudly across Tower Green until she came to the scaffold.

There, the executioner was waiting for her. They placed a bandage over her eyes. She groped for the block saying:

'Where is it? What am I to do?' Then, as she laid her head on the block she said:

'Lord, into thy hands I commend my spirit.'

The Tower is as rich in stories of intrigue and violent death as any building in the world. Although there are no more Royal prisoners in the Tower, and it is no longer a place of execution, there are many things that have remained unchanged for the past 900 years.

Every night at precisely 9.53 p.m. the Ceremony of the Keys takes place.

The Crown of England – and all the regalia used by the Sovereign at the Coronation – is still kept at the Tower.

The famous ravens still flutter across Tower Green as they did on that morning in June when Jane walked to the scaffold. In those days they were a common sight in the streets of London, and were protected because they were very useful as scavengers. There were no Corporation dustmen in those days and the ravens ate up all the rubbish. There is a superstition going back to Charles II's time that if the ravens ever leave the Tower – both the Tower and the Empire will collapse.

Today it is Yeoman Quarter Master Henry Johns' special responsibility to look after the ravens. He has six birds officially 'on the strength', and he draws three shillings per day per raven to buy horse meat to keep them fed. The ravens' wings are clipped so that they can roam as they please in the Tower grounds, but will never fly away and place the Tower in jeopardy.

The Yeomen of the Guard are the official custodians of the Tower and there are 40 of them. On special days. like the Queen's Birthday, they wear splendid uniforms of scarlet and gold. Their everyday 'undress' uniform is in blue and red. But the famous beefeater hat is always worn, and on ceremonial occasions it is adorned with red, white and blue ribbons.

A detachment of the Brigade of Guards helps the Yeomen to protect the Tower. There can be no chances taken with security because the Crown of England, the Orb, the Sceptre and all the priceless regalia used by a sovereign at the coronation, is still kept at the Tower of London.

Every night for the last 700 years, the Chief Yeoman Warder and the guards have taken part in the Ceremony of the Keys.

At 9.53 p.m. precisely, the Chief Yeoman Warder locks up the gates of the Tower. He returns with the key, escorted by soldiers under arms. When the party reaches the Bloody Tower, they are challenged by the sentry on duty.

'Halt – who goes there?'

The Chief Warder replies

'The Keys.'

'Whose Keys?' demands the sentry.

'Queen Elizabeth's Keys,' replies the Chief Warder.

The sentry lifts his bayonet and says:

'Pass, Queen Elizabeth's Keys. All's well.'

The little party continues until it meets the main guard. The officer of the Guard gives the order:

'Guard and Escort – Present Arms!'

The chief warder then doffs his Beefeater hat and says in a loud voice:

'God bless Queen Elizabeth.'

'Amen,' respond the guard and escort.

The massed buglers blow the last post, and another day ends in the age long history of the Tower of London.

The case of the miniature emperor

John says 'Can you solve this case? Who stole the priceless miniature? There are five clues here – see if you can spot them.'

A 999 call sent Sergeant McCann speeding to the Waterloo Museum. Within the last ten minutes, a priceless miniature of the Emperor Napoleon, in a jewelled frame, had been stolen – and a man lay bleeding by a shattered glass case.

The Curator, Dr Muirhead, was waiting anxiously on the steps when Detective Sergeant McCann and his constable arrived.

'Who's the injured man?' asked the Sergeant, as the Curator hurried them along the silent corridors to the little gallery where the theft had taken place.

'He's Professor Allerann, from Leipzig,' said the Curator – 'he's an expert on Napoleonic relics, and if anything serious has happened to him, it will be an international tragedy – far worse than the loss of the miniature.'

'What was the picture worth?' asked the Sergeant.

'It was priceless – quite irreplaceable,' answered

the Curator, 'but I'd had it specially insured for £20,000 – the value of the jewels that surrounded it.'

When they reached the gallery, a white faced Professor Allerann was lying back in a chair whilst Reynolds, a St John Ambulance man, gave him first aid.

'There you are, sir,' he said, 'I'm sure you'll find that sling very comfortable.'

'How is he?' asked Dr Muirhead.

'Not bad, Gov,' said Reynolds, cheerfully. 'He's had a nasty crack on the head with a cosh and he must've broken his arm when he fell. But it's only a compact fracture and he'll be right as rain in no time.'

'That's good news,' said Dr Muirhead. 'When I heard him cry for help and rushed in, I thought he was seriously injured.'

'Then you were first on the scene of the crime,' noted McCann.

'Yes, that's right, Sergeant,' replied the Curator. 'And when I saw him lying there surrounded by broken glass, I shouted for the St John Ambulance man. We always have one on duty here.'

'You didn't see the thief then?' questioned McCann.

'No, I didn't,' said the Curator.

'First time I've been on duty here,' chipped in Reynolds, 'and this has to happen!'

'Did *you* see anything suspicious?' McCann asked him.

'Yes, I did! I was on duty in the main vestibule, and just before Dr Muirhead called, a man rushed past me down the steps.'

'Did you notice anything unusual about him?' queried the Sergeant.

'Not specially. He was a young, thick set chap. He was wearing jeans and a leather jerkin. And – oh yes – he was carrying a briefcase.'

'A briefcase,' said McCann. 'That's odd. He doesn't sound like a business man. Did the professor see him, too?'

'I don't know,' said Reynolds. 'You'd better ask him.'

'Is he well enough to question?' said McCann. 'He looks very pale.'

'Oh yes, sir – provided you don't go on too long. He's suffering from shock. He was unconscious when I found him so I gave him a good stiff brandy – he should be all right now.'

McCann moved across to the white faced Professor.

'I'm sorry to bother you, sir,' he said, producing his identity card. 'Sergeant McCann, Scotland Yard. If we're to catch this thief, I really must ask you one or two questions.'

'But of course, Sergeant,' said the Professor,

weakly. 'I will do anything I can to help catch ze thief.'

'First of all, can you give me a description of the missing miniature?'

'It vas a beautiful portrait of ze Emperor Napoleon as a young man – one of ze earliest photographs ever taken of him.'

'And what about the frame?'

'I cannot tell you. It vas covered mit jewels and set in gold, but naturally ze frame is not interesting to a dedicated student of ze great Emperor.'

'Could you describe the picture to me, sir?'

'It vas splendid! Zere stood ze Emperor in his finest uniform – but wizoot ze hat!'

'I see, sir. Was he wearing his eye patch?'

'No. It vas before he lost his eye at Waterloo zat zis picture vas taken.'

'What about the thief, sir? Did you get a look at him before he attacked you?'

'Only for a moment,' sighed the Professor. 'He vas a young man mit a leather coat.'

'That confirms the description I've already got,' said McCann. 'Thank you for your help, Professor. Would you mind giving me the name of your hotel, in case I need to question you further?'

'I regret, Sergeant, zat I leave tonight for Leipzig. I catch ze night boat train from your King's Cross Station, and tomorrow I shall be in Paris and half way home. In fact, I must be leaving right away. If you have finished your questions, Sergeant . . .?'

McCann closed his notebook with a snap.

'No more questions, Professor. But I have one favour to ask.'

'Zertainly . . .?'

'Would you be so kind as to take off that sling and bandage?'

At once Reynolds leaped forward.

'As a medical orderly I'm afraid I can't permit you to interfere with my patient,' he commanded.

'As an officer of the law, I'm afraid I must insist,' snapped McCann, ripping off the sling.

There was a flash of light as the small jewelled portrait dropped from the bandages. 'The miniature!' gasped Dr Muirhead, 'but I don't understand . . .?'

'It's perfectly simple, sir. Hold that man,' he rasped to the constable as Reynolds leapt for the door.

'These men are two of the most accomplished jewel thieves in Europe,' said McCann, as the handcuffs were snapped home. 'Between them they've made five very careless mistakes – and this time – just like Napoleon – they've met their Waterloo!'

Did you spot the mistakes? John did. Check your answers on page 76.

Biddy Baxter, Edward Barnes and Rosemary Gill would like to acknowledge the help of Gillian Farnsworth and Margaret Parnell. Designed by Baker/Broom/Edwards

Answers

Hello There

1 This model is an exact miniature, on a one-sixth scale, of the Fouler BB 1 Plough Engine.
2 Trying out the 'Blue Peter' sledge on an artificial snow slope. The 'snow' is made of thousands of tiny plastic wires.
3 Taurus, the performing bull, walks downstairs with his owner Colin Newlove. Taurus can also sit and curtsey.
4 This Aircraft Crash Rescue Truck is used by the Royal Air Force at airfields all over Britain.
5 High in the roof of the 'Blue Peter' studio, Flight-Sergeant Terry Allen of the Flying Falcons gives John some Free Fall parachuting instructions.
6 The Tug-of-War team from Berwick in Sussex – total weight 120 stones – train by pulling against this 67 h.p. tractor.
7 Rosa – or Radio Operated Simulated Actress – a radio controlled robot invented by Bruce Lacey.
8 A pumpkin, weighing 159 lb., was used to make this giant Halloween Lantern.
9 Coylum Marcus, the £2,000 champion cat, came to the studio with a detective to guard him.
10 John fights it out with Barry Paul – Junior Foil Champion of 1968.
11 650 feet up the mast at Crystal Palace.
12 Demonstrating a scale model of the gas rig 'Mr. Louie'.
13 Fanhill Faune, a very friendly dalmation, and Crufts 1968 Supreme Champion.

Puzzles

3 Valerie, Richard, Michael (or Rachael), Annette, William (or Gillian)
4 Baby, Balls, Bat, Bathing costume, Beach, Birds, Boat, Bonnet, Boy, Breakwater, Brolly, Bucket.
5 Daisy, Violet, Crocus, Tulip, Rose.
6 Television Programmes (Prize, Rivulet, Orchestra, Glide, Request, Architect, Multiply, Minimum, Escalator, Squander).
7 Holly.
8 (c) Wasp
9 Have you tried our competition yet?

The Case of the Miniature Emperor

1. Reynolds was obviously not a genuine St John Ambulance man. He said the Professor had a *compact* fracture. There is no such thing. A first aider would know that the proper description is *compound* fracture.
2. Reynolds said he gave the unconscious Professor brandy. Again, this proved he was a fake. A first aider would never give a drink to an unconscious person, or risk giving a stimulant like brandy in a case of shock.
3. The Professor described the miniature as 'an early photograph of Napoleon.' This proved he was not an international expert on Napoleon as photography was not invented in Napoleon's life time.
4. The professor said the picture was made before Napoleon lost his eye at Waterloo. Napoleon never lost an eye in a battle. (It's Nelson, not Napoleon, who wears the eye patch.)
5. The Professor said he was going to catch a boat train to Paris from King's Cross Station. King's Cross Station has no cross-channel boat trains.

Acknowledgements

'The Best Christmas Tree of All' and 'Father David's Deer' were illustrated by Robert Broomfield.
'Bleep & Booster' and 'Bengo' were illustrated by 'Tim'.
'The Widest, the Highest, the Greatest!' was written by Dorothy Smith
'Destination Moon' was by Geoffrey Wheeler.

All photographs in this book were taken by Charles Walls, with the exception of the following:
Ski-ing photographs, pages 9–11, by H. Schwarzler; Alan Oliver, page 44, and Crown Jewels, page 72, by Central Press Photos Ltd.; The Tamar Bridge, page 61, by permission of the 'Daily Telegraph' and all other pictures on pages 60–61 by Radio Times Hulton Picture Library; Lady Jane Grey, page 70, by permission of the National Portrait Gallery; Ceremony of the Keys, page 72, by Barnaby's Picture Library; Competition photograph by Joan Williams.

Blue Peter Competition

Would you like to meet Valerie, John, Peter and the rest of the 'Blue Peter' team? Would you like to see all the animals? Would you like to come to London and have tea with them all? This is your chance!

Since our last 'Blue Peter' Book, there have been 84 editions of 'Blue Peter', and Valerie, John and Peter have done 588 different things between them. But each of them has a favourite – Can you guess what it is? If you can, write it down on the entry form – but remember, it mustn't be what *you*'ve liked best, but what you think Valerie, John and Peter have enjoyed doing the most.

The First Prize will be an invitation to an exciting

Blue Peter Party

and there will be lots of competition badges for all the runners up, too.

First Prize winners and runners up will be notified by letter. The closing date for entries is 10th January, 1969.

Send your entry form to: Blue Peter, BBC Television Centre, London W12. and mark the envelope *Competition*

Entry form	Signed	Age

Address

Valerie's favourite

John's favourite

Peter's favourite